LIVING
QIGONG

LIVING QIGONG

THE CHINESE WAY TO GOOD HEALTH AND LONG LIFE

JOHN ALTON

Foreword by Donald R. Fowler, M.D.

SHAMBHALA
Boston & London
1997

Shambhala Publications, Inc.
Horticultural Hall
300 Massachusetts Avenue
Boston, Massachusetts 02115
http://www.shambhala.com

© 1997 by John Alton

9   8   7   6   5   4   3   2   1

Designed by Ruth Kolbert

First Edition

Printed in the United States of America

♾ *This edition is printed on acid-free paper that meets*
the American National Standards Institute Z39.48 Standard.

Distributed in the United States by Random House, Inc.,
and in Canada by Random House of Canada Ltd

Library of Congress Cataloging-in-Publication Data

Alton, John, 1954–
Living qigong: the Chinese way to good health and long life /
John Alton; foreword by Donald R. Fowler. — 1st ed.
p.   cm.
Includes bibliographical references.
ISBN 1-57062-106-3 (alk. paper)
1. Ch'i kung.   I. Title.
RA781.8.A48   1997   96-47018
613.7'148—dc21   CIP

Krishna: I fought against terrible powers and I did what I could.

—Jean-Claude Carriere's *The Mahabharata*, "Krishna's Death"

When one does not incur small diseases,
one will not incur moderate diseases.
When one does not incur moderate diseases,
one will not incur serious diseases.
When one incurs no serious diseases,
one will never die.

—Taoist Aphorism, *The Great Tao*

Like a shipwreck we die going into ourselves.

—Pablo Neruda, "Nothing but Death"

CONTENTS

Part Two

THE EIGHT MOVEMENTS OF THE THREE EMPERORS QIGONG

FOREWORD

In April of 1988, I was fortunate enough to be selected as a member of the first fitness delegation to the People's Republic of China. The members of this American delegation came from a wide variety of disciplines, including medicine and surgery, physical education, physical therapy, chiropractic, athletic training, administration, nursing, exercise physiology, special education, health promotion, basic research, coaching, and employee health. The project was characterized by an open exchange of information about our professional activities, our cultures, and our histories. This interaction was essential since to view China's system of fitness and health, one must be familiar with the value system of the Chinese, which so strongly influences their approach to fitness.

I entered into this adventure with an open and curious mind. Too often we Westerners forget that our knowledge of medical science spans a period of two hundred years, whereas the Chinese have been in the business of healing for some four to five thousand years. They must be doing something right to have survived for all that time. One cannot help being awed by the sight of thousands of people in the parks in Chinese cities at 5:30 each and every morning, faithfully going through their Taiji and Qigong routines. I'm certain that not all of them understand completely the medical ramifications of such actions, but their culture has encouraged these practices. This, I believe—from a physical, emotional, and spiritual per-spective—constitutes the purest form of preventive medicine.

Our delegation visited numerous hospitals, observed storefront clinics, and spent time in the universities and martial arts institutes. Unbeknownst to me, at that time John Alton was in Beijing studying with a martial arts and Qigong master.

By the time I returned to the United States I was convinced that tradi-tional Chinese medicine had something to offer us here in the West, and I wished that I were a bit younger so that I might take the time necessary to learn Chinese and study the traditional medicine. Soon my busy practice of surgery again consumed me and my thoughts of this other pursuit dimmed—that is, until I read an announcement in the local paper that our recreation department was sponsoring a summer class in Taiji. The instructor was John Alton, and his credentials impressed me: he had a long-standing martial arts background, he had been a college instructor in English, and he had spent two years in China training under an accom-plished master of martial arts and Qigong.

Now, after several years of instruction and training in Qigong, I am certain of the potential value of traditional Chinese medicine in our mod-ern society. As you will learn in John's book, the Chinese approach is premised on a force called *qi,* which is considered the basis of health and well-being. *Qi* is cultivated by the repeated practices of martial arts such as Taiji and of Qigong meditation.

One of the reasons that Chinese medicine seems so alien to us in the West is that its system of thought and practice, developed over thousands of years, does not easily lend itself to our techniques of scientific investiga-tion. It has its own perception of body, health, and disease, and it has its own vocabulary. However, in the end, Chinese medicine and Western medicine are both talking about how to effectively treat the same diseases. I see a great potential power in combining the best of both of these worlds.

As you will learn in this book, there seems to be some common denomi-nator, referred to by the Chinese as *qi,* which I feel must work through, stimulate, or maintain our immune system and which in return is responsi-ble for the well-being of our bodies both in sickness and in health. Only recently have we discovered drugs that can stimulate our immune systems and help the fight against cancer. The Chinese seem to have discovered some similar phenomenon several thousand years ago, but have carried it a step further and postulated that the free flow of *qi* throughout the body is the basis of physical, emotional, and spiritual health. Taiji and Qigong allow this to happen naturally and thus become their basis of preventive medicine. Only recently, in our discussions of cradle-to-grave health care, have we here in the West begun to truly emphasize the value of such preventive maintenance.

Like all things of value, the ability to control this force does not come easily and may never come to some. There is potentially, however, something in it for everyone. Just as the majority of the Chinese in those parks each morning probably do not understand the philosophy and years of development behind their practices, they nevertheless are receiving the benefits of their ancestors' efforts. We too can benefit, even without completely understanding, if we are willing to expend the effort.

DONALD R. FOWLER, M.D., F.A.C.S.
Chief Medical Officer
Augusta Medical Center
Fishersville, Virginia

ACKNOWLEDGMENTS

This book represents a long, strenuous effort involving both the direct and indirect influence of a lot of people. First, I am sincerely grateful to my teacher and Chinese friends who made my experience in China the life-altering adventure that it was. Stateside, special thanks to John Hughes for providing the drawn illustrations and to Mike Bryan for the photographs. Don Fowler and Chic Thompson gave a lot of encouragement and some good suggestions; David "Geronimo" Germano guided me through the forest of Buddhist and Hindu sources; and Todd Kissam, Linda David, and Denton Brosius boosted me over the word-processing hurdles. Additional thanks to Herbert "The Professor" West for introducing Alfred Korzybski, as well as to Frank and Patt Hobbs and Ben Green for suggesting Paramahansa Yogananda. Elizabeth Philpott and Ge Xue helped me in ways I'll never be able to repay, and my best friend and student John "Doc" Dokken, as well as my other loyal friends and students, deserves much praise for working hard to help Qigong take root in their hearts and in their culture. Final and deepest thanks to Cynthia Adams-Alton for her patience and suggestions throughout the ordeal of writing this book and to my editors, Peter Turner and Kendra Crossen, for their careful, attentive effort to make *Living Qigong* live.

Pronunciation Key

This text uses the pinyin (pronounced "peen-yeen") system of transliterating Chinese words into romanized letters. Broad phonetic spellings are given below for the corresponding Chinese words.

Bagua Zhang = bah-gwah jahng
bai hui = bye hwee
Bajiquan = Bah-jee-chwan
Changquan = Chahng-chwan
Chen = Chun
chong mai = chong my
da zhou tian = dah joe tee-an
da zhui = dah jwee
dai mai = die my
Dalian (city) = Dah-lee-an
dan tian = dahn tee-an
dong gong = dong gong
dou dong = doe dong
du mai = due my
fu = foo
Gongfu = Gong-foo
hui yin = hwee yeen
jian mai = jee-an my
jia ji = jee-ah jee

jin ye = jeen yeh
jing = jeeng
jing gong = jeeng gong
jing luo = jeeng l-woe
ke = kuh
koutou = koe-toe
lao gong = la-ow gong
mai = my
ming men = meeng mun
Pigua = pee-gwah
qi = chee
qi zhong = chee jong
Qigong = Chee-gong
qing gong = cheeng gong
ren mai = rin my
shan zhong = shahn jong
shen = shun
Taijiquan = Tie-jee-chwan
tiao dong = tee-ow dong

tudi = too-dee

wai = why

wei lü = way lew

wushu = woo-shoe

xiao zhou tian = shee-ow joe tee-an

xin = sheen

Xingyiquan = Sheeng-ee-chwan

xue = shweh

Yang = Yahng

yin/yang = yeen/yahng

you haizi = yoe hi-zuh

yü zhen = yew jun

yun shou = yewn show

zangfu = zahng-foo

Zhong Guo = Jong Gwoe

zi fa dong = zuh fah dong

zu qiao = zoo chee-ow

NAMES

Chao = Chow

Fu = Foo

Liang Shuming = Lee-ahng Shoe-meeng

Liu Ziping = Lee-oe Zuh-peeng

Mao Zedong = Ma-ow Zeh-dong

Yan Xin = Yee-an Sheen

Zhang Jinwei = Jahng Jeen-way

Zhang Xue = Jahng Shweh

Zhi Xiaomeng = Jur Shee-ow-mung

INTRODUCTION

At the beginning of 1987, things were looking down. My marriage had recently ended. My contract as an English instructor at the local university was about to run out. I had written my first novel but couldn't find an interested publisher. I had only a handful of people I could call friends, and relations even with them were often strained and hypocritical. In addition to these personal gripes, I felt oppressed and marginalized by "Reaganomics," which hadn't been especially kind to lower-level faculty at American universities.

By late spring the job search had turned up a few prospects but nothing I felt like jumping for joy over, so on a lark I applied for a Fulbright to Taiwan. For good measure I fired off a few confident letters to mainland China, in particular to Beijing University. That summer I got an invitation from China's Ministry of Education to work there for a year, compiling and editing English textbooks to be used in most of China's major universities. I accepted at once.

Going to China may have been more an act of desperation than the fulfillment of a dream, but I held the vague hope that China would be a new start. I savored the irony that three hundred or so years earlier, fed-up Europeans had traveled to America with a similar vague hope.

Along with my economic and personal miseries, I was nursing a wrist that had been broken two years before. It happened in 1985: a bike wreck, during which I landed on my right hand and fractured the navicular scaphoid, one of the most difficult bones to heal because in a great many cases it is poorly supplied with blood. For a year I had gone without treatment, relying on my general practitioner's diagnosis that the wrist was badly sprained. The second year I spent in a series of casts with built-in electric coils, designed to stimulate blood flow to the site of the injury. At least two of the orthopedists I saw wanted to operate, but they weren't able to guarantee more than a fifty-fifty chance of recovery. By the time I left for China, the bone had not yet mended. The orthopedist I ended up with prescribed another six to twelve months in a cast. I opted for a plastic brace and signed a waiver agreeing in effect not to sue the orthopedist, who warned me that removing the brace before another six months could prevent the bone from healing.

I had no reason to doubt my doctor. He was a no-nonsense surgeon who specialized in reconstructing the shoulders, knees, and ankles of athletes. But after two years of failure I had a nagging suspicion that I had reached a wall with Western medical science. My only hope, I decided, lay in China.

My reason for bestowing such faith on China was simple: my fifteen-year involvement in Asian martial arts. For two of those years I had specifically concentrated on Chinese martial arts and medical practices, such as acupuncture, herbology, and Qigong (also often transliterated as Chikung), the practice of working with *qi*, the Chinese word for "air," though it means something closer to "life force." My teacher at that time—a white man who had lived in Taiwan for two years—treated me with Chinese herbs and acupuncture, and he promised even greater results if I would move to San Diego where he lived so he could treat me regularly. That option died when I couldn't find a decent job there. With the invitation to work at Beijing University, however, I could get treated at the source, and the Chinese government was footing the bill.

When I arrived in China, I had to undergo a battery of health tests, during which I asked my Chinese doctors if they could heal my wrist with acupuncture or herbs. The resounding and disappointing answer was no; the break was too old. A few doctors suggested that I try Qigong, which wasn't exactly heartening. I had been doing Qigong for two years, and it hadn't done a thing for my wrist. At that time Qigong was at a pinnacle of popularity throughout Beijing. There were many "masters" offering classes both at the university and in neighboring parks. One campus Qi-gong master had a thousand students in his class. As a foreigner with an "incurable" health problem, I had exotic appeal to the fairly large number of available masters. During my first three weeks, I worked with four different Qigong masters, and throughout my two-year stay in China I met many more; and each of them claimed to have "the best" Qigong. In spite of this plethora of teachers, I ended up working for two years with only one man. This wasn't an easy decision, as I was constantly promised better results by rival Qigong masters. As it turned out, I did the right thing. When my teacher found out that I had turned down other offers in order to remain his student, he took me deeper into his confidence and his method. In the competitive world of Qigong practice, loyalty is perhaps the greatest gift a student can give the teacher.

Ultimately, the disappointments and naive hope that drove me to China became assets once I began studying Qigong in earnest. Stripped of the usual blandishments of self-worth, I came to China and Qigong credulous, enthusiastic, and sincere. In *Alive in the Bitter Sea*, sinologist Fox Butter-field observes that in the former glory days of imperial China, only for-eigners who recognized China's superiority by bringing gifts to the emperor were allowed to live and trade in its coastal ports. I had brought no gifts, but I did carry in my heart a conviction that I was in a land whose greatness exceeded that of my own. This conviction permeated my every action for the first six months or so of my two-year sojourn. That was no small accomplishment. The typical long-term Western reaction to the mainland can only be characterized by degrees of loathing and horror. While I also felt these things, my original mind-set, together with the expe-riences that mind-set opened, enriched my reactions to China and contrib-uted to a deep sympathy for its people. I finally left China on a tide of international revulsion, only a few days after the government soldiers crushed the Democracy Movement, but I never abandoned the sense that China held some of the world's greatest secrets about life and death. That the very key to health and longevity resides in a land of staggering confu-sion, sickness, and death remains one of the world's great ironies and paradoxes.

By the summer of 1988, I had learned enough Chinese to communicate on a basic level with my Qigong teacher, who was so pleased with my progress that he invited me to journey with him to the northeastern coastal city of Dalian where he was going to conduct a two-week seminar for a teacher's college. In the thick of summer, we left Beijing around midnight by train and stayed up most of the night talking and eating watermelon seeds. The "hard sleep" car was smoky and crowded with passengers who were curious to see and converse with "the foreigner." One passenger, a small, stocky man with a silver crewcut, seemed particularly fascinated with me, especially when he found out that I was learning Qigong and *wushu* (a general term for the Chinese martial arts). He sat with us for over an hour, and though most of the time I had to rely on my teacher's wife as translator, the man kept his eyes on me, with a broad, authentic smile constantly on his lips. Our talk was rambling and extensive, but the part that stuck with me was his fixed certainty that something great was going to emerge from the fusion of the cultures of China and America, which to many Chinese was a synonym for "the West." "If I were your age," he said, "I would take the best ideas from China and the best ideas from America and I would create something. I would raise a child up by those ideas."

The notion that the merger of America and China would produce something marvelous was widespread among many Chinese I met, especially the young. In a way, the Democracy Movement was probably the tragic fruition of the great hope expressed by the silver-haired man. With this book I hope to reclaim some of that hope for the fusion of East and West, but here the fusion is based on morality and health, not on economics, politics, and social issues. If this book can provide readers with a greater understanding of how to control physiological processes that are currently unreachable, if it can help readers see that longevity, within certain limits, can be as manageable as sound financial planning, then it will have accomplished much. But I have even higher hopes. This book strives to clarify and outline a method of achieving what Paramahansa Yogananda in his *Autobiography of a Yogi* called "the householder yogi," a powerful spiritual person who remains an active social, political, and economic participant. Other cultures have names for people who achieve this sort of transcendence. Buddhists would use the term *bodhisattva*; Native Americans, *shaman*; Christians, *saint*. Qigong offers yet another approach to a similar goal.

Part One

LIVING QIGONG

1

ENCOUNTERING MY TEACHER

I FIRST MET ZHANG JINWEI IN LATE OCTOBER ON AN athletic field near the southern wall of Beijing University. He was conducting a sword class on an empty volleyball court beside a dirt running track. A compact Chinese man of about five feet, eight inches, Zhang wore a blue jogging suit that zipped up the front, and a happy, Buddha-like expression lit up his square face. He stood before twenty or thirty Chinese and foreign students and led them through a series of maneuvers, thrusting and turning with his sword, the blade rattling from the force of his movements, which seemed to project entirely from his broad thorax. After the class ended, I snagged one of the students as a translator and moved in for a direct conversation. Zhang's face beamed with ruddy vigor, his eyes large, darkly radiant, and kind. His black hair was short and combed neatly. He seemed simultaneously young and old, having a mature, sturdy bearing in the chest and shoulders, but unlined, smooth-shaven skin with a rosy sheen that reminded me of a healthy child's flushed cheeks. After the introduction, Zhang asked what I wanted from him. Through my translator I explained that I wanted two things: martial arts training and my wrist healed. Zhang nodded once and said quickly and quietly that he could cure my health problem with Qigong. I should come to his room that night at seven-thirty.

That night I showed up at Zhang's building with a young student who had been assigned by the university to help me. His name was Zhi Xiaomeng, a thin, willowy twenty year old who wore his hair in short bangs and was dressed in a natty white shirt and dark slacks. Bicycles filled the entrance to Zhang's building. The cement floor was wet and slimy, and the scent of urine was stronger than in any of the Chinese dorms I had visited so far. We climbed the dimly lighted stairs. Garbage had been swept into neat piles in the corners, and the halls of the first two floors were jammed with furniture and mysterious items covered with tarpaulins, voices of all ages ringing and echoing, sourceless, omnipresent. Zhang was waiting at the top of the stairs, still dressed in the blue jogging suit. He led us down a hall into a tiny room whose entire space was consumed by a bunk bed, desks, shelves, and a table, leaving a narrow passage in the middle. In the very back was the bunk bed, where Zhang's wife sat knitting, their five-year-old daughter beside her. His wife's name was Liu Ziping (wives keep their own names in Communist China), and she had a very round face, healthy white skin, large eyes, and full lips. Her hair resembled a billowy black helmet. The daughter, Zhang Xue, wore thick, Christmas-red pajamas, her hair shaped like an upside-down bowl. Within minutes I discovered that Liu Ziping was fluent in English and that I hadn't really needed Zhi's help as a translator after all. As it turned out, Liu proved indispensable to my training. Without her help, it would have been impossible to understand much of Zhang's teachings.

Near the end of the visit, which had been more of an intimate introduction and interview than an actual lesson, I asked Zhang how he was going to heal my wrist. He reached over, tore off the Velcro straps, slid the brace off my forearm, and tossed it in the corner. At first I was terrified, but I told myself that taking off the brace one time wouldn't hurt anything. Next Zhang asked both Zhi and me to stand and hold out our arms as though gently embracing someone. Zhang stood up, switched off the overhead light, and turned on a lamp sitting on the desk. Zhi translated phrase by phrase. "Relax," he said, "close your eyes, and try not to think about the outside world." I did as I was told, but I couldn't help keeping my eyes cracked, the lamp glow an island of light in the dark sea of the room, Liu Ziping and Zhang Xue still sitting on the bed, quiet and unmoving as statues. Zhang moved behind me, and suddenly my body became hot, not uncomfortably so, but distinctly enough for me to notice. My chest felt as though it were expanding, filling with something almost ticklish, joyful. My right wrist began to twitch involuntarily, my fingers tingling, itchy. Then I realized Zhang was standing beside me, his hand hovering over my right forearm.

Zhang spoke, and Zhi told me to open my eyes and lower my hands and make the palms face one another, then bring the hands together, then bring them apart. To my surprise I felt not only warmth but a magnetic sensation, which I had felt before when doing Qigong both back in the States and in China, but this time the sensation was stronger and with a greater difference in quality. When I separated my hands, there was a pulling sensation, as though magnets were attracting each other, and when I brought my hands together, the force pressed outward, as though the polarity had reversed itself.

The effects of this first Qigong treatment from Zhang were dramatic. After one month of Zhang's treatments, I could kill the common cold, or at least eliminate the symptoms. Five months later, without the aid of any medicines, braces, casts, or therapies other than Qigong, my wrist was completely healed.

During that time I ferreted out some details about Zhang. In the early to late 1970s he had been one of China's top martial arts athletes, whose training and prowess are far different from that depicted in Kung Fu movies from Hong Kong and Taiwan. On the mainland, martial artists are hand-picked at an early age by scouts who attend various competitions around the country. The selectees are then sent to "physical culture institutes," where they live in dorms and train both mentally and physically in a college curriculum of wushu and Qigong. Zhang was inducted into the Beijing Physical Culture Institute when he was sixteen, but he had been training since childhood. Zhang's whole family, which was from the northern countryside of Beijing, had been martial artists, the primary influences being his paternal grandfather, a Taoist, and his uncle, a Shaolin Buddhist. They fought for control over Zhang. He learned from both, but he finally became a member of his grandfather's school because his grandfather's "internal" wushu was more powerful than his uncle's "external" wushu. Like most experienced American martial artists, I thought I was familiar with the distinctions between the internal and external mar-

5

tial arts. "Internal" wushu was slow and soft and reputedly helped the practitioner to develop qi. The form I had studied in the States, Xingyiquan (literally "form-mind fist"), was internal. "External" wushu was harder and more rigorous. Supposedly Karate, in which I had two black belts, derived from Chinese "external" wushu.

Though I assumed that Zhang meant his grandfather's wushu had fighting power superior to his uncle's, I was surprised to learn that Zhang was actually referring to his grandfather's Qigong, which cured him of pernicious anemia. At age ten Zhang had developed the disease, and after his case had been pronounced hopeless by Beijing doctors, a friend and training partner of Zhang's grandfather took him into the countryside to work with the grandfather's master, who prescribed a daily regime of Qigong, wushu, and a few herbs. In two years all traces of the disease vanished. When I looked into what Western medicine had to say about pernicious anemia, I learned that it would have taken chemical treatments of the blood to lead to any kind of satisfactory result. Mere exercise, according to Western medical canon, couldn't have provided a cure. Even more incredibly, one effect of pernicious anemia would have been premature aging, such as gray hair. Zhang's hair was jet-black, and his face was as unlined as that of a man in his mid-twenties. Despite a slight paunch, Zhang could turn a complete flip with a sword and land in a split. At age forty, he could perform impeccably 126 different forms of wushu.

Zhang never hesitated to give credit for all this to his Qigong, a practice he claimed to carry a daunting obligation. I asked him to elaborate, and he told the story of two Qigong students—one a training partner of Zhang's teacher, the other Zhang's fellow student—who abused their practice and "were punished by heaven." When I asked how they were punished, he answered with a flat, "They died." Zhang told me this fairly early in our association, so I tended to dismiss the comment as a bit of high drama designed to rattle a foreigner. But by the end of my second year, I began to understand what he meant. After seven years of teaching Zhang's method in the United States, I make a point to mention to all my students the story of the two practitioners who "were punished by heaven." My students tend initially to think I exaggerate, just as I thought Zhang exaggerated. If they continue their training, they come to know better.

2

THE
MIDDLE WAY

URING MY FIRST FEW WEEKS AT BEIJING UNIVERSITY, A
visiting professor of Chinese philosophy introduced me to a thesis by Confucian scholar Liang Shuming that greatly enhanced my understanding of Qigong. In an effort to define Chinese culture, Liang proposed a cultural spectrum between two great extremes: India and the West. The West, according to Liang, is an external culture, focused on material success, dominance of nature, and "evidence," bits of lasting truth apparent to the five senses. At the other extreme, traditional India represents internal culture, eschewing the sensate world as an illusion, succumbing utterly to nature rather than attempting to conquer it. China sits between these extremes, a culture that seeks harmony with nature rather than dominance or submission. Liang was referring largely to China's potential for harmony due to Confucianism, in conjunction with Taoism and Buddhism. The influence of these three traditions has been so strong in China that even the purgations designed by Mao Zedong couldn't eradicate them.

Liang's thesis steered me toward looking broadly into parallel practices in India and the West: yoga and science respectively. The general philosophies behind yoga and Western science provide points of both contrast and comparison with Qigong. While yoga, Western science, and Qigong may be vastly complicated subjects, each meriting lengthy treatment,

Liang's cultural spectrum helped me to appreciate each practice as a human endeavor, rather than that of a particular race or society, and to view Qigong as a synthesis of disparate elements, a middle way.

According to Liang's thesis, yoga should reflect an inward orientation, a turning away from the external world in favor of a richer, internal one. Though there are many forms of yoga, some of which differ sharply, its overall view of the external world draws largely from the Hindu concept of *maya,* which defines sensory existence as an untrustworthy, disappointing place to which people are confined for the sole purpose of evolving to more enlightened, nonmaterial levels. Yoga assists the practitioner in evolving toward these higher levels.

One form of yoga that is particularly helpful with regard to understanding Qigong is *kriya,* which focuses on the breath to access *prana* (primal internal energy), then through long and hard practice brings this energy up from the base of the spine to the head. In so doing, the practitioner eliminates bad *karma* (errors from previous lives) and speeds his or her evolution to a higher plane. The alternative is reincarnation in the realm of maya. In this way, devout kriya yogis spend their lives cultivating their spirit in preparation for the afterlife. Each is a self-contained universe, whose dependency on the material world is merely temporary. According to Paramahansa Yogananda, a leading authority on kriya yoga, success depends on two things only: having a guru or master and practicing kriya yoga. Of these two necessities, obtaining a master is the hardest. Yogananda contends that yoga masters intuitively select their disciples. It is not enough for the potential student to show devotion. The master knows the disciple by inner vision. If lucky enough to be selected, the novice must undergo a period of testing, which in Yogananda's case lasted ten years. At the end of this testing period, the master imparts energetically the ability to experience high-level kriya yoga. At that point the disciple must use the method of meditation to enhance the master's gift.

Western science, on the other hand, is a practice born of Middle Eastern religion and Greek Hellenism. In fact, natural philosophy, the ancestor of modern-day astronomy, physics, and chemistry, sprang up within the medieval Christian church and eventually leaped over the walls to form its own church: the modern university, whose architecture even today resembles the fortress design of its forebear. Since then, Western culture has used science to grapple with and improve external life. The molecular and subatomic sciences have added immensely to our understanding of many natural secrets, and this understanding has resulted, at least in the short run, in longer life. Science improves the human condition by building houses, roads, vehicles, and technologies so that we experience a better quality of life.

Science approaches human longevity in a similarly pragmatic way. Once the cardiovascular system became identified as the key mechanism for determining strength, vitality, and speed, aerobic training—such as running and swimming—for half an hour, three or four times a week, became the prescription for good health. More recently, evidence on the benefits of proper diet, flexibility, and recovery has altered the scientific definition of *fitness,* but a total consensus remains elusive. A substantial amount of verifiable proof must be amassed before science can place its stamp of approval.

As Western culture has developed, it has placed higher premiums on science. Having a scientific mind might be disparaged in certain academic and artistic communities in the West, but there is no denying that, in general, having a scientific education can lead to a "better quality of life." The prosperity of doctors and scientists far exceeds that of most other professions, with the exception of law and politics, which is less exception than corollary. Both law and politics incubated with natural philosophy in the early church's sacred womb of reason. And with the onslaught of the electronic "communications revolution," even lawyers, judges, and politicians find themselves subsumed by computer technology, one of science's greatest creations.

As far as internal life is concerned, science doesn't offer many answers. It offers no opinions on life after death and seems reluctant to embrace its possibility. In fact, its relentless commitment to studying and improving the external environment has inadvertently undermined the religious institutions it came from. Those institutions represent the West's response to the internal questions of the afterlife, and, broadly speaking, the answers are external in character. The human soul is not bound exclusively to the physical, corruptible body, which dies and allows the soul to leave. In Christian and Muslim traditions, the perfected soul enters Heaven, an otherworldly existence usually thought to exist in the physical sky. Hell, the opposite of Heaven, is generally characterized as a descent into punishment and is traditionally associated with being underground. In Judaism, the central spiritual goal is to bring the Messiah into the external realm, which then becomes a paradise for all souls, living and dead. Liang's thesis that the West is compelled to the external appears to ring true even in the case of death.

Like Indian yogis and Western theologians, Qigong practitioners had to answer questions about what became of this inner world after death. Exhibiting an external bent, they concluded that the body ought to be maintained for as long as possible and so looked to nature for models of lastingness. They saw that animals hibernated in winter and that slow-moving creatures like the turtle lived a long time. They gazed at trees and saw the way they endured from season to season, far exceeding the life span of an individual human. From these observations, they then turned inward with the conclusion that the examples of longevity found in external nature lay potentially inside the body.

The functioning of Qigong's inner world generally resembles that of kriya yoga. Like kriya, Qigong uses breath to access primal bodily energy (*jing*), then circulates that energy throughout the body in three basic configurations. But Qigong also has an active component that works much like the aerobic exercises touted in the West. When practiced in conjunction with meditation, Chinese martial arts, or *wushu,* becomes a form of external Qigong, demanding the flexibility emphasized by some schools of yoga and the cardiovascular and muscular stamina of Western sports such as track and field. Thus, in an effort to satisfy the demands of both inner and outer nature, Qigong produced a concept of fitness that reflects a balanced concern for both the internal and the external.

When the various languages by which science, yoga, and Qigong characterize themselves become a point of focus, science differentiates itself from the other two practices. The language of science is rooted in the mathematical properties of numbers and the laws of geometry, which scientists must master in order to master science, an effort that extends beyond learning differential equations and quantum theory to keeping abreast of the latest research that pours out of university laboratories, science foundations, and government agencies in a ceaseless flood. By learning to manipulate the language of science, a person earns the pinnacle

Ph.D. or M.D., or both, which then permits entry into high-level science.

Though yoga certainly has a rich verbal content (particularly in the *Mahabharata,* the Upanishads, and the Vedas), it is first and foremost a physical practice. Like yoga, Qigong subordinates language to practice. The founding of Qigong is generally credited to primitive Taoists. Later, Buddhism and Confucianism incorporated certain aspects of Taoist Qigong into their own systems, just as Indian Buddhists and Muslims absorbed some Hindu yogic methods. In China today there are many different "schools" of Qigong. Some are Taoist; some are Buddhist; some are Confucian; some are all three. Most of the people who practice, and I would hazard to say most of the teachers, don't spend their time reading esoteric Taoist or Buddhist texts. Most aren't licensed to practice acupuncture or prescribe herbs, functions performed by the external arm of the culture. They may have some basic knowledge of Chinese medicine, but the main thing these people know is that if they practice correctly and adequately, they can control their health. This is to say that unlike mastering Western science, benefiting from Qigong doesn't require a supreme command of the vocabulary by which Qigong describes itself, just as it is not necessary for the kriya practitioner to master the *Mahabharata* in order to gain from the practice of kriya yoga. Like kriya yoga, profound success with Qigong depends largely on two things: a good teacher and devoted practice.

In response to the verbal barriers that separate science, yoga, and Qigong, I answer with the epitaph, "The map is not the territory," an expression coined by the Polish mathematician Alfred Korzybski to emphasize that language and dynamic physical reality are not the same things. Just as some maps are accurate and others aren't, so too are all efforts to verbalize or write about that reality. No matter what, a map is never the piece of land, and a group of words is never the subject of discussion. This is an extremely important point regarding Qigong and the way it differs from both Indian yoga and Western science.

11

3

SWIMMING
ON LAND

DENG MING DAO, AUTHOR OF *THE SCHOLAR WARRIOR* and *The Chronicles of the Dao,* asserts that all exercise involving rhythmic breathing is a form of Qigong, hiking and swimming being among the best. This follows from the literal meaning of *qigong.* The word *qi* in its general sense means "air," and the Chinese word *gong,* from which *Gongfu* (Kung Fu) is derived, means working over a long period of time to develop skill. In this sense all exercise is a form of Gongfu. Western walkers, joggers, swimmers, golfers, weight lifters, gymnasts, and players of tennis and other ball games are technically engaged in some level of Qigong. Though such exercisers may never feel their own qi, they can certainly enjoy the effect of qi through better health.

The Chinese exercise considered most closely related to Qigong is Taijiquan (Taiji for short)*—the slow-motion martial art that reigns as China's

---

*In deference to China and its numerical hegemony, in this book I use the alphabetic system the Chinese created for transliterating ideograms into Indo-European letters. That system is called pinyin. The other common system for transliterating Chinese is called Wade-Giles, which often leads to misconceptions and mispronunciations, especially where Taijiquan is concerned. Wade-Giles uses the spelling *T'ai Chi Ch'uan,* which causes people to confuse the Wade-Giles term *ch'i*—the equivalent of *qi*—with the Wade-Giles term *chi,* which in pinyin is written as *ji* (and pronounced *gee,* as in "gee whiz").

Figure 1. *Yin/yang diagram, also known as the taiji diagram.*

most popular form of exercise. Because of China's sheer numbers, Taiji ranks as the most popular exercise in the world. The literal translation of *Taijiquan* is "great extremity fist," partly because Taiji fighters were notoriously "great." But the word for extremity—*ji*—bears additional comment. When used in the word *Taiji*, it can refer to a remote border of existence, where flesh becomes spirit, capitulated in the *yin/yang* diagram. The curved line separating the dark and light halves of the yin/yang diagram is said to represent the *taiji*. This definition brings *taiji* closer to the meaning of Qigong, where yin and yang merge as a single energy.

Many Chinese refer to Taiji as "swimming on land." The analogy proves more literal than figurative. After all, the air that surrounds us is a fluid similar to that found in oceans, lakes, and streams. When we move, our bodies slice through our fluid just as fish swim through the water. Generally speaking, we are not aware of the surrounding air unless a strong wind blows or if we run fast or stick our heads out of moving vehicles. But we can also become sensitive to the air by moving slowly, as in Taiji. Most Qigong practices involve at least in part the kind of slow motion seen in Taiji movements. By moving slowly, the Qigong or Taiji practitioner begins to feel the way the body's heat and biochemical energy interacts with the surrounding air. This same medium conducts every energy wave and particle that hurtles in from outer space or rises up from

13

the ground. It is alive with the constant effusions of nature; it is also alive with the constant effusions of human and animal life.

Once the Qigong practitioner is able to sense his or her body's thermal and energetic interaction with the air, he or she has entered the water, so to speak, and begun to dog-paddle. Dog-paddling is nice and can be fun for a while, but the dog-paddler doesn't get to experience the true dynamics or depths of the water. By learning more sophisticated strokes, the dog-paddler evolves into a true swimmer, capable of longer, more rigorous swims, which in turn invigorate the swimmer. With greater lung capacity, the swimmer can dive underwater and see a whole world that was invisible on the surface. With proper gear, the swimmer can become a snorkeler or even a scuba diver, acquiring more and more the attributes of a water creature.

Unfortunately, few Qigong practitioners get beyond dog-paddling. They may learn a few Taiji-like moves from a video or a book or a six-week class at the local college, and think that is all there is to Taiji or Qigong. They don't realize the profundity beneath, which, like the sea, holds as much danger as it does beauty. The more competently one swims, the greater the chance of enjoying the beauty and avoiding the danger.

If the novice Taiji practitioner dog-paddles, the novice Western exerciser flails. Of course, Western exercise can make a person stronger or feel better, but too often the Western exerciser follows the external reflex with maniacal obsession. When exercisers show improvement in terms of speed, strength, or stamina, they feel "good" for "making progress," even though they may in fact feel sore knees, ankles, and back, to name a few common symptoms of such standard Western exercises as jogging, tennis, and basketball. If we frame such behavior with the metaphor of swimming, the limits become even clearer. Imagine a muscle-bound man with rippling pectoral and biceps; now imagine this man trying to swim laps in a pool. Straining to keep his head above water, he thrashes wildly to the other side of the pool, where he clings to the wall and rests, gasping. His heart rate goes up, his muscles get worked, but he doesn't get the full benefit of the water. Such an approach to exercise is not only ungainly, it is unhealthy. Evidence of this has been mounting since the exercise explosion of the early 1970s. Sold on the belief that health means getting the heart rate up and keeping it there for sustained periods of time, athletes like Jim Fixx ran—and continue to run—themselves into the grave. Others run themselves into crippling leg or back injuries. Convinced that being "in shape" means measuring less flab, many discover after a time that they are addicted to working out.

In the past decade there has been a profusion of sports medicine practices, which may be due in part to growth through research and a simple increase in the number of exercisers. Still, the increase in sports medicine means that more people began exercising and hurting themselves prior to or during the growth period. An increase in the number of people exercising might account for a growth in the number of sports injuries among novice exercisers, but it doesn't explain the problems incurred by veteran sports enthusiasts, who ought to know better. Among the many athletes I have observed, known, and worked with professionally—whether in running, tennis, racquetball, cycling, football, basketball, track and field, weightlifting, aerobic dance, golf, or, ironically, swimming—I see constant examples of excessive exercise. If they aren't nursing shoulder, leg, or back injuries, these excessive exercisers suffer from depleted immune systems, drained constantly by both the stress of exercise and ordinary life.

Swimmers Who Can't Swim: Martial Arts in the West

Swimming as a metaphor for exercise produces a striking oxymoron. Imagine, if you will, competitive swimmers who "can't swim," that is, swimmers so manic about their performance that they destroy their health. Many Western practitioners of Asian martial arts find themselves in such a predicament. Their art, or rather the way they practice their art, leads not to health but to destruction. Although there must certainly be a number of good schools of Asian martial arts in the United States, Canada, Europe, and other places besides Asia, the general tendency of most schools is to focus excessively on the fighting aspect of the tradition. Martial arts journals scarcely examine this tendency, and I find that most American martial artists are deeply offended when this emphasis is questioned.

The causes of the Western corruption of Asian martial arts are rooted in the evolution of the martial arts in Asia. In China, martial arts emerged from two places: the monastery and the military. The monastic martial arts—Taoist or Buddhist—were wedded to meditation and Qigong practices, which the military tended to ignore, unless the practices showed some immediate benefit in warfare. Other areas of Asia, most notably Japan and Korea, recapitulated this schism and after World War II passed it along to Western nations, where Asian martial arts went on to be developed, often by former military personnel.

Like most other Western martial artists of the 1960s and 1970s, I began my training under these historical conditions. Though David Carradine's television series and the astounding development and skill of Bruce Lee filled me with desire to practice Kung Fu, the only martial arts I could find initially was Japanese Shoto-kan, founded by Gichin Funakosi, the father of modern Japanese Karate. Next I tried Korean Tae Kwan Do, which I perferred to Shoto-kan because it emphasized the kind of fancy kicking I had seen in Bruce Lee movies. I ended up studying another Korean style, Tang Soo Do, in which I eventually earned a black belt. Tang Soo Do was popularized by Chuck Norris, and even more than Tae Kwan Do, it encouraged high, acrobatic kicks. When I began, the skill it took to leap up into the air and throw a spin kick attracted me, but I very rapidly became absorbed in the most pervasive aspect of American martial arts: contact sparring.

At first I thought of contact sparring the way Howard Cosell defined boxing: more honest than all the other civilized games that needed balls, rackets, clubs, and abstract rules to disguise the reality that two or more people were engaged in an effort to dominate each other. By the time I had earned my green belt, however, I began taking pleasure in beating other men, especially if they were cocky. Later, in my thirties, with another black belt in another style, I had added youthfulness to my reasons for wanting to beat an opponent, a kind of perverse recompense for my own aging. By the time of my wrist injury, I had joined the ranks of the other seasoned black belts. In the *dojo,* or practice studio, we bowed politely before drubbing people we didn't respect. We lived like aging gunfighters, ceaselessly challenged by testosterone-oozing eighteen- to twenty-five-year-old males. At the same time there was the next level of the pecking order to teach and police: less developed men, women, and children, who either beat up on one another or competed through *kata*s, brief explosive routines of choreographed movements with martial applications. As though enough adrenaline weren't already involved, there was sexual intrigue: attractive young women seeking power through Karate, only to become cheerleaders or concubines for the more libidinous male black belts.

Not every *dojo* I have trained in was as bad as the one I've described, but these problems are all too common. One of the things that can prevent a Karate school from getting out of hand is the huge attrition rate. Most people won't put up with repeated beatings; they usually quit. A statistic that I often heard invoked was that out of all the people who study Karate, only two percent ever earn a black belt. Whether or not that statistic is true, it is rare that an instructor has the charisma and physical stamina to sustain a large student enrollment. I have belonged to three American schools where the instructors were able to maintain large, steady student bodies, and I have observed several others. In all cases, the schools resembled cults or abusive families. Nobody said anything bad about what went on, and anyone who quit was immediately condemned. The schools were closed societies with semipermeable walls, lobster traps where getting in was much easier than getting out. Some argue that schools run by Asian-Americans are different. I have found this to be only partly true. Most high-level Asian-American instructors I have met and trained with have at some point demonstrated a propensity to be as domineering as the worst American instructor I have encountered.

The two great problems that undermine the majority of martial arts schools are an overwhelming devotion to competitive violence and a negligible concentration on the more refined practices born of the monastic martial arts. Under no circumstances does a human being enjoy getting punched in the face, ribs, and stomach; nor does one relish broken, jammed, sprained, twisted, or contused extremities and joints. The most honest response to such afflictions is rage, especially if inflicted by someone whose defeat is the object of the game. But rather than honestly express this rage, the Karate student is taught to bow and feign politeness and respect. If the student is vanquished, he or she must accept defeat

17

humbly, which is easier to do if there aren't any injuries. But the longer a student participates, the more likely injury becomes. As skill improves, so does zeal, which often leads to accidental loss of control, which in turn leads to a punch in the head, a finger in the eye, a foot in the groin, a whack on the shin, and so forth. Then rage becomes a part of the student's life. In many cases rage can be provoked simply by losing a sparring match, whether or not there was any pain.

Most Karate instructors have evolved through the ranks under such conditions, which leave both mental and physical scars. To expect spiritual enlightenment in such an environment is to expect a man to grow fat in a desert. As a result, many Karate "masters" become masters of deception. Like cult figures or abusive parents, they bully and confuse their wards, not out of sadistic pleasure but out of their own confused efforts to maintain their facade and to remain in control.

I don't outline this archetypal perverse Karate master to degrade martial arts. I do so to illustrate a point: inside every exercise addict there is a similar set of impulses at work. The violence of the Karate master's environment simply exaggerates the harmful effects of competitiveness from which many Western athletes suffer.

To return to the original metaphor, such people don't know how to "swim." They don't know how to practice Qigong. Still, there is plenty of evidence that wise and modest exercise—including Karate—can contribute greatly to health. Heart patients and diabetics, to name two, have been able to reclaim their health through basic, sensible exercise. Heart muscles grow stronger, metabolic rates improve, blood flows to the extremities, and sweat cleans out the pores of the skin. Improvement in each of these systems enhances other dependent systems. For example, increased blood flow to the extremities enhances *collateral circulation:* the body's ability to generate new capillaries to muscles and skin (a very important effect of deep-level Qigong practice). Though they may not feel the bioenergetic interplay between body and air, people who exercise, diet, and emote within sensible limits do better than either dog-paddlers or flailers. If they were shown the proper method, they could feel the "charged" quality of the air around them. They most resemble Qigong practitioners of modest accomplishment, who move through the waters of life with a kind of graceful breaststroke or elementary backstroke.

Swimmers, Snorkelers, and Scuba Divers

So what about those who practice deeper levels of Qigong? How do they train? How do they think? First, they don't regard exercise as a competitive endeavor. If they're not as fast or as strong as they were the day or week or month before, they don't mind. They accept their performance level as the best they can do under the circumstances. The deep-level Qigong practitioner also never questions the need to rest and recover from vigorous exercise. All explosions of energy are followed absolutely with Taiji and meditation. Without recovery, aerobic exercise becomes after a period of time an *enervating* rather than an *innervating* experience. Qigong practitioners know that aerobic exercise is to the body what rainfall is to crops. Rain makes crops grow, but after a certain point, the crops drown. A final, most important attribute of the deep-level Qigong practitioner is an awareness of the subtleties of physical existence. This awareness begins with the ability to "dog-paddle," the ability to sense the bioenergetic interactions of the body and the air. With devout practice this awareness grows and uncovers greater subtleties until it becomes irrefutably clear that life is both moral and spiritual. This recognition doesn't derive from the words of books or the speech out of people's mouths; it derives from the experience of training and carrying that experience into the realm of everyday living.

So the question becomes: how to practice Qigong? Or in terms of the swimming metaphor: how to increase "swimming" competence? Again, books and videotapes and six-week Taiji classes aren't enough. The student must obtain a good teacher and practice for a period of time in the teacher's presence. This isn't easy. As with yogis, Qigong masters pick their students carefully according to strict moral and spiritual standards. Moreover, practicing with the teacher isn't a simple matter of having movements and facial expressions corrected. During practice the teacher transmits qi through the hands, fingers, head, or whole body into areas of the student's body. The student can receive in specific places, such as the lower back and top of the head, or can absorb the teacher's qi through the pores of the skin. In either case, this is how the student progresses from dog-paddling to swimming. Granted, there may be one in a million who is so virtuous or lucky as to progress on his or her own, but, generally speaking, without a teacher who willingly imparts qi, the student is stuck in the dog-paddling stage.

As the swimming metaphor implies, Qigong is a multilevel discipline. Students who simply learn movements without receiving qi from an accomplished teacher—no matter how long they practice—won't get far beyond breaststroke. With the right teacher, however, students can learn to freestyle, backstroke, and butterfly.

These difficult, rigorous strokes find their counterparts in the external Qigong of wushu. Performing wushu is much like swimming intervals of the various racing strokes. The heart, lungs, and muscles get a physical workout, but more important, the body's qi, which follows the blood, is raised to a highly energetic state. At that point, qi and blood can be regathered with Taiji movements, which is like doing a slow elementary back- or breaststroke. Then the qi and blood can be stored and circulated with sitting meditation, the equivalent of snorkeling. Longer meditations amount to scuba diving.

Through the above analogy, I have just outlined Zhang Jinwei's Qigong method, which is like the curved line of the Taiji diagram, dividing Indian yin from Western yang. Like Western aerobics, Zhang's wushu builds muscle and conditions the cardiovascular system, and his Qigong meditation helps calm and clarify the mind and imparts a feel for spirituality, much as the practice of yoga is reputed to do.

Both external wushu and Qigong are essential components in the equation of health, but only Qigong meditation is constant. Once deep-level Qigong is achieved, any form of aerobic exercise (including swimming) can be substituted for external wushu. But wushu should never be dropped completely, because it does far more than increase flexibility and stimulate the cardiovascular system. Many of the postures and movements of external wushu are simply more rigid, speedier versions of those found in Taiji, itself a form of Qigong. Like Taiji, then, external wushu can facilitate the flow of qi in the body, specifically to the extremities and outer musculature. The able-bodied Qigong student can benefit greatly from practicing a suitable form of external wushu and should make it part of his or her regimen. For older or infirm Qigong students, the practice of Taiji or other forms of "internal" wushu suffice.

4

THE FIRST TIME
BELOW THE SURFACE

Aﬀter nearly a month of steady work with my teacher Zhang, I was set back one day by a bad cold that had infected everyone else in the building where I lived. My head felt as though it were covered with a fishbowl filled with murky water, my sinuses clogged, my eyes watering. China is one of the disease centers of the world, and infection among foreign residents there is a way of life. During my two-year stay, my fellow foreigners were eaten alive by one upper respiratory infection after another. That cold night in mid-November would be the last time a germ had its way with me. That night I went "snorkeling."

In the evening, when it was time for Qigong, things went their usual course. Zhang led me through a series of Taiji-like moves, then had me stand with arms held in the posture of gentle embrace for ten minutes or so, during which time I was supposed to let my body move at the waist if I felt the urge. In the previous weeks I had developed a routine of turning slowly at the waist, back and forth. I was so relaxed that unconscious contractions in the muscles of my lower back and abdomen pulled first to one side, then the other, causing me to rotate slowly, pausing for a few seconds on the left before turning automatically to the right. During part of this time, Zhang moved around behind me, injecting qi into various parts of my body, especially my wrist, which always felt better after every Qigong class.

After standing meditation, we got down on the floor in half-lotus positions for the sitting meditation, or *jing gong* (literally "still" or "silent work"). While sitting, I was supposed to gently pressure random thoughts out of the mind by imagining a red line moving up and down the front of my body, but if a powerful image presented itself, I was to allow it to linger and develop on its own. I was also supposed to record in a journal my reactions to the meditation and tell Zhang about any particularly striking visions that arose. During the time I had been practicing with him, I'd had only one to report. A week earlier I had seen myself at the bottom of a big cave, but high above was a huge opening, a brilliant burst of light shining through, the rocky entrance becoming clouds, a hole in the sky revealing the burning sun. When I told Zhang about the image, he expressed what seemed for him a lot of enthusiasm. Later, his wife translated his elliptical response that "something is going to happen soon." Though cheered that Zhang had spoken positively about my practice, I was secretly irritated by his vagueness. He explained very little about the things he taught, insisting that I "shouldn't think too much about things." I didn't have the faintest idea why I was imagining a red line running up and down the front of my body. From what I knew, Qigong meant moving qi around the entire body. That was what I had read in books and had been taught in the States.

Those were the very thoughts going through my head when suddenly a spasm erupted just below my navel, a wild pulsing my body had never experienced. The pulse shot immediately up into my head, popping my sinuses so that a gush of mucus flowed from my nostrils. The pulse moved up from below my navel to my head with the inhale, and descended back with the exhale to where it began. My cold symptoms vanished.

A few weeks later I woke up one morning again with a stopped-up head and a scratchy throat, which made me think at the very least that my previous Qigong experience had limited value, but then I went through the routine again, and the pulse leaped from below my navel to my throat, where the pulse stayed seemingly on its own, the soreness beginning to localize in the right submandibular lymph node. After I had endured a few minutes of continuous throbbing, the soreness moved like a living creature to the left submandibular lymph node, pursued by the pulse, which chased the sensation back to the right, then back to the left, the soreness lessening each time, until it dissipated. Then the pulse went straight to the center of my forehead, my sinuses popped open, and the cold symptoms had faded by the time the session was over.

From that point on, Zhang had my full attention. Though I continued to question and doubt some of the things he said—a habit, I should add, that merely slowed my progress—I began rearranging my emotional and conceptual priorities. Rather than assuming that I already knew a lot through my education and martial arts background, I started to feel, like Hamlet, that there are a lot of things in life that most people haven't even dreamed of yet. The skeptic in me gave way to the conviction that Qigong was not just a "feel good" meditative exercise but a profound method of accessing unconscious bodily processes.

Acquiring a pulse below the navel, bringing up that pulse with the breath to the middle of the forehead, and then allowing it to descend to the navel upon the exhale is a necessary condition for doing advanced Qigong. Oddly, in all the magazines and books I've read on the subject, I find next to no mention of this phenomenon. Yet according to Zhang and judging by my own experience, the pulse below the navel marks the start of deep-level Qigong. Zhang refers to the pulse as *you haizi* (literally "have child") and offers a thoroughly Taoist medical explanation, but the phenomenon can also be approached from a Western physiological perspective.

The Descending Aorta, the Iliac Vessels, and the Lymphatic System

One possible explanation for the lower abdominal pulse that occurs during Qigong has to do with the functioning of the descending aorta: the thoracic and abdominal portions of the aorta, the major blood vessel that branches from the heart both up toward the head and down toward the lower region of the body. The descending aorta drops from the heart to the lower abdomen where it splits off into the iliac vessels that supply the legs and the feet with blood. When a relatively slim person lies face up,

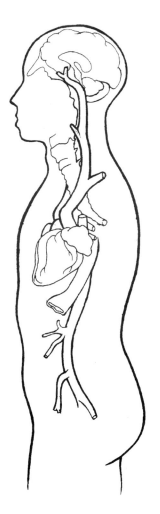

Figure 2. *Descending aorta.*

the pulse is usually visible on the abdomen above the navel. The entire aortic system is an important blood vessel because it links the kidneys, heart, and brain with a great river of blood. Controlling the aorta, perhaps through some subtle physiology of the descending aorta, would mean controlling the blood supply to those three important organs. Since all healing and bodily growth take place as a consequence of blood flow, such control is unarguably desirable.

Moreover, the immune system is dependent not only on the flow of blood but also on the lymphatic system, which ramifies throughout the body in its own network. The lymphatic system is complex but generally follows the path of the arteries. By means of both blood and lymph, immune bodies reach and attack infections. All disease persists because blood and lymph fail to do their job.

Joining the complex network of blood and lymph vessels in the lower abdomen is an even more complicated bundle of nerves radiating off of the lumbar and sacral areas of the spine. Only the brain itself possesses a greater nervous reticulum. Because of this abundance of nerves, some medical professionals refer to the lumbar and sacral nervous formation as the "abdominal brain." Perhaps the lumbar and sacral nerves, combined with the descending aorta and accompanying lymph glands, constitute a potential psychosomatic system that Western medicine has either ignored or misunderstood.

Deep-level Qigong may conceivably provide a way of both controlling and understanding this ill-defined "system." By accessing the nether regions of the nervous system in order to control the aorta and the accompanying lymph nodes, the practitioner may very well be able to direct the immune system to attack with precision the site of an infection.

A practitioner of deep-level Qigong can easily demonstrate the phenomenon of you haizi by letting an observer both watch and palpate the pulse's movement up and down the body. I do this all the time to show students what they should hope to attain through their practice and to deter the wide-eyed naiveté with which many students approach Qigong. Unconsciously driven by Western culture, they are in love with abstraction, image, and language, which, as Zhang continually warned me, can be impediments to progress in Qigong. Many forms of meditation—including several popular forms of Qigong in the United States—rely on elaborate imageries, sounds, smells, ceremonies, and paraphernalia. Contrast such practices with Zhang's stark red line, which symbolizes the extent to which the mind should be involved in Qigong.

Spontaneous images or visions, however, often signal important developments in the first level of deep Qigong practice. The vision I had of seeing a light from the bottom of a cave, Zhang later informed me, falls into a broad category indicating that Qigong will have a spiritual impact

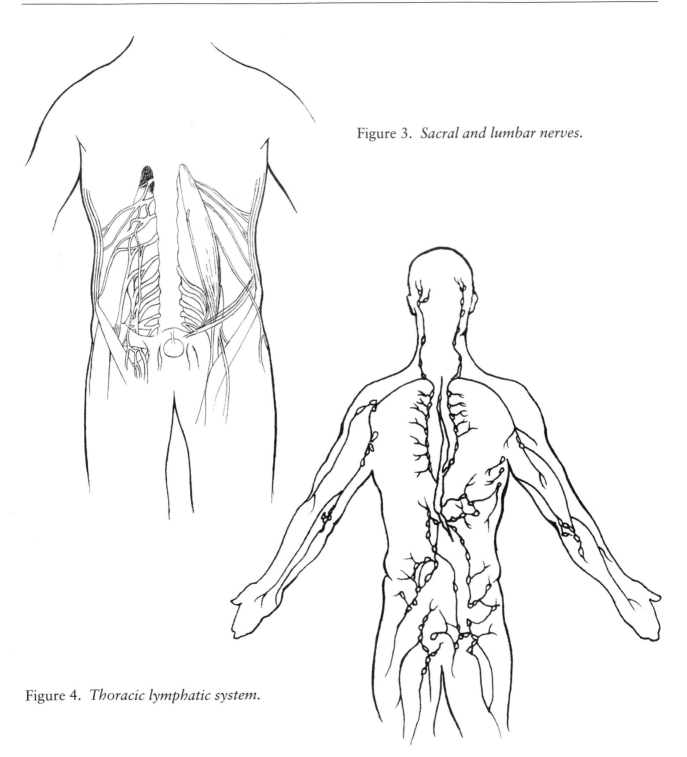

Figure 3. *Sacral and lumbar nerves.*

Figure 4. *Thoracic lymphatic system.*

on the practitioner. Zhang calls this category of visions the "big room," because the practitioner frequently sees him- or herself seated on the floor of a cathedral-like room. Another common signal image is that of a tube running up and down the inside of the body. I had this impression also, but never mentioned it. A beginning meditator sometimes becomes disoriented and forgets the things that come to mind. Other mental reactions, such as communicating with dead relatives, seeing colored lights, smelling vivid odors, or hearing odd sounds may have particular significance for the individual student. Such reactions generally point to some psychological or psychosomatic difficulty that the student should take note of. But above and beyond any thought or image that pops into the head, the somatic response of the lower abdominal pulse is primary, the first great step toward managing health. It marks the ability to control the circulation of blood, lymph, and immune bodies.

Controlling blood and lymph flow permits health benefits far beyond accessing the immune system. Bruises, sprained joints, and broken bones all heal as a result of blood circulation. In fact, the failure of my own circulatory system—along with a year of reckless abuse—prevented my wrist from mending. The doctors had told me that my wrist suffered from avascular necrosis, which basically meant that part of the bone was dead from lack of blood supply. Once I attained the pulse in my lower abdomen, however, Zhang instructed me to use my breath to bring the pulse up to my collarbone. From there I focused my mind to conduct the pulse down my right arm, directly to the injured wrist bone. I did this with relative ease. After every session, my wrist, which ordinarily ached and registered a sharp pain if moved, felt noticeably better. Five months later, I was doing handstand push-ups.

It is difficult to convey just how miserable losing the use of my wrist had made me without detailing the place exercise occupied in my life. Before breaking my wrist, I could do one hundred push-ups on my knuckles. I did twenty-five pull-ups at a time and practiced gymnastics a couple of times a week. I ran five or six miles and swam a thousand yards three to five times a week, cycled twenty miles a day on weekends, and practiced Karate three or four times a week. Perhaps now it seems clear why I can speak about exercise addiction with a certain amount of authority. For two and a half years my ability to do those activities had been compromised to the point of vanishing. I couldn't do a single push-up with both hands. My wrist was so damaged that using my hand to lean against the wall sent a shock of pain up into my shoulder and neck, both of which were so swollen from inflammation and so misaligned from compensating for the injury that one doctor thought I had damaged my upper spine.

Since the bone failed to heal because of a lack of blood, it stands to reason that through Qigong I increased the blood supply to the injured site. It may be that Qigong accesses some aspect of collateral circulation, one of the key benefits of aerobic exercise. Over the years, as my Qigong proficiency has progressed, I have been able to similarly treat other parts of my body injured through wushu and accidents. These experiences, along with those of students, lead me to believe that deep-level Qigong bestows the power to open collateral capillaries. If this is true, then many assumptions about supposedly "irreparable" areas, such as knees and even the spine, may be incorrect.

One of my students, a former U.S. Navy SEAL who was nearly killed in an underwater explosion in the Middle East during the mid-1980s, serves as a striking example. When Lenny first came to train with me, I noticed that he walked with a limp. When I asked him about this problem, he revealed an extraordinary story of courage and will. After the explosion, Lenny was clinically dead for about twenty minutes. Though he was revived, he remained in a coma for five weeks. When he finally regained consciousness, his doctors told him he would never walk again. For two years he was confined to a wheelchair. Then one day his love for the water provoked him to get in a swimming pool, where he discovered he could barely move his legs. After two more years, he managed to walk under his own power, but his balance was poor, and he had to take medication to prevent seizures and treat depression. He also suffered from migraine headaches and insomnia. Because his doctors prescribed steroids, he put on a considerable amount of weight, which further depressed him. Though he had regained the use of his legs, his doctors assured him that owing to "irreparable" nerve damage to his head and spine, he would never feel on one side of his body, the side of his limp. Once a magnificent specimen of raw physical power, Lenny was now overweight and disabled at the age of thirty-one. The first thing I did was show Lenny the aortic pulse, then I let him feel my qi. At once his face lighted up, and he happily reported that he did indeed feel "something." From Lenny's enthusiastic reaction, as well as from his other remarkable traits, I knew he would make good progress.

After five months of doing only Taiji, Lenny's balance improved dramatically. He also was able to stop taking his medication for depression, he lost over thirty pounds, and recovered forty percent of the sensation in his formerly numb side. His migraines and insomnia vanished. When Lenny began his Qigong training, he experienced a few predictable setbacks. Since Qigong opens the unconscious mind, many of Lenny's former combat traumas came back to haunt him, dampening his spirit and discouraging regular practice. The doctors told Lenny that because of his head injury his face would remain numb, and for several months it looked as if their prediction would remain true. Lenny could feel his lower abdominal pulse and could make it move up to his chest, but he had no sensation in his forehead. Then, after several weeks of regular Qigong practice, the pulse suddenly appeared in the middle of his brow. At about the same time, his mental and physical capacities noticeably increased. He was suddenly able to learn more difficult movements more swiftly than before and is now training in more physically demanding Chinese martial arts. Not bad for a man who was given no hope of ever using his legs again. As time goes by, I expect even greater improvement in Lenny. Even more important, *Lenny* expects to improve.

Though I have never been measured with instruments while doing deep-level Qigong, I'm certain it could be done. Even so, that would only prove that I can control the circulation of blood (and conceivably lymph as a consequence). Such a test would do nothing in terms of proving that qi exists, the major thrust of Western research on Qigong. As of yet, no Western scientist has produced definitive proof of qi, and on these grounds many dismiss Qigong. This is at least in part a semantic, cultural problem. And while physicians and physicists shake their heads skeptically over the failure of Qigong to "prove" itself, proficient practitioners sit quietly, circulating their pulses, destroying infections at will, and prolonging their lives.

5

QI

AND THE WEST

ONE OF MY QIGONG STUDENTS, WHO ALSO HAPPENS TO be a good friend, was asked once how his Qigong practice was going. "The jury's still out," he replied curtly. This student had experienced the lower abdominal pulse and even managed to move it vaguely from his lower abdomen up his body to his head. Still, he couldn't bring himself to believe in Qigong.

The details of this student's experience epitomize Western science's frustrated efforts to study and understand Qigong. Fittingly enough, his education includes an advanced degree in mathematical logic. Whenever he experienced something extraordinary, he first searched for an explanation that would in effect normalize the experience. Failing that, he tried to discount the phenomenon as the "power of suggestion" or the "placebo effect." Finding a possible Western corollary explanation, such as the anatomy of the aorta, made him feel better, but it wasn't enough. He insisted that the phenomenon be repeatable. If the phenomenon failed to repeat, or if it seemed to lessen in some way, his skeptical guard came up. His mind full of doubt, he wasn't able to concentrate very well during meditation, which led to unsatisfactory results. After repeated failure, he lost interest in maintaining the practice. The claims my more successful students and I made about the miraculousness of Qigong could all be attributed to "mass hysteria." If Qigong works, he might say, it works only because the individual wants it to work. Stroking a cat, some studies have shown, can decrease blood pressure and thus contribute to better health. Why not, then, simply purchase a cat?

An essential preconception in the Western medical approach to treatments for disease is that the treatment should work regardless of whether or not the patient believes the treatment will work. This preconception underlies the practice of double-blind studies, in which patients are divided into two or more groups and given different treatments for a particular ailment. Group members and their doctors don't know what kind of treatment they are receiving. Sometimes one group receives no treatment; instead, they are given a placebo. In this way Western scientists determine which treatments work and which don't.

Though double-blind studies generally help verify or dispel a treatment's worth, they also suggest that the patient's attitude can influence treatment. Until very recently, Western medical research has regarded the patient's attitude as either irrelevant or problematic. But as Dr. Deepak Chopra points out in *Quantum Healing*, practicing physicians generally have a positive regard for their patients' attitudes. They often encourage their patients' belief because past experience shows patients are more likely to recover if they believe they can get well.

Chopra explores the conundrum created by this fascinating split between Western medical science practice and theory through the example of cancer patients, whose bodies are effectively poisoned through radiation and chemotherapy. This "scorched earth" approach to cancer treatment evolved out of double-blind research and the assumption that the patient's mind or will has little to do with treatment. Statistically speaking, survival rates of cancer patients who receive radiation and chemotherapy are as good as or better than those of patients using available alternatives, which include treatments that involve the patient's will. Chopra questions why Western medical science focuses so obsessively on the broad statistical picture instead of on the exceptional patients who completely recover without radiation or chemicals, and he argues that Western medicine should be enlisting, not neutralizing, the patient's mind. To accomplish that enlistment, he offers the practice of Transcendental Meditation. Chopra convincingly integrates details on DNA research to suggest that the entire body is intelligent. Through the mechanism of DNA and bio-chemical "communicators" called neuropeptides, every cell of the body can theoretically communicate. Transcendental Meditation is a way of accessing and controlling the body's communication potential, much as the first step to deep-level Qigong accesses and permits control of the cir-culatory system.

Again the problem of belief enters the picture, and up pop Western objections about the power of suggestion and the placebo effect. The stance of Western medical science toward Chinese medicine, acupuncture, herbology, and Qigong has been one of habitual skepticism. Over the past twenty or so years since mainland China reestablished connections with the West, Western researchers have formed a body of opinions that run the gamut from excitement to rejection, averaging out to lukewarm interest. Acupuncture and herbology seem to have captured the greatest attention, largely, I suspect, because they are external methods. So far as Qigong is concerned, however, the jury is still out.

A notable effort to comprehend Qigong occurred in the early 1980s when a young medical student named David Eisenberg went to Beijing to study traditional Chinese medicine for a year. Eisenberg recorded his experiences in his book *Encounters with Qi* and more recently appeared as co-host on a segment of Bill Moyers's PBS series *Healing and the Mind*. At the conclusion of the television segment, Moyers asked Eisenberg if he had ever felt or experienced qi in all of his ten years of research. Eisen-berg's disappointing answer was no, but he was quick to add, as he did in his book, that more research needed to be conducted to find out if there was anything to Chinese medicine or the theory of qi.

In *Encounters with Qi*, Eisenberg described several demonstrations of qi, but each time he insisted that the demonstrations be repeated. When the repeated demonstrations failed or the results were lackluster, he reluc-tantly fell back on the explanation that whatever he saw or felt the first time was due to the power of suggestion, the placebo effect, or "mass hysteria."

Eisenberg's efforts illustrate why Western science continues to fail to understand Qigong. The first reason stems from scientific research's knee-jerk reflex to have results duplicated. Such a reflex is at complete odds with the nature of Qigong, which by nature involves the human ability to amass qi within the body to maintain health. Not only is this ability difficult to obtain (*gong* means "skill developed through rigorous practice"), but once attained, it is easily lost. Once a Qigong master exudes qi, that qi is gone and can only be rebuilt through considerable effort.

When Eisenberg described the times that Chinese projected qi into his body, what he said he felt—vibrations, warmth, tingling—are all sensations that students report when they begin the practice of Qigong. The sensations were enough to arouse Eisenberg's interest and curiosity, but he had no way of proving for himself whether he really felt something or whether the sensations were created by the power of suggestion. In a more flamboyant example, he met in a public park a Qigong practitioner who claimed to be able to light a fluorescent bulb with his hands. Eisenberg, who was hosting Harvard professor Herbert Benson and several other American doctors and scientists, invited the Qigong practitioner to meet the group later across town and demonstrate his ability. Most Westerners who visit China receive special treatment and so never come to understand how exhausting life can be for the average Chinese, travel being among the most enervating aspects. Eisenberg and his guests seemed completely unaware of this when the man showed up looking bedraggled and drained. In fact, he had caught an upper respiratory infection since meeting Eisenberg in the park. Still, the man valiantly tried to show the Westerners his skill. After several tries, during which he shut the door to darken the room and rubbed his hands together, he finally succeeded in lighting up a fluorescent bulb with his hands. Eisenberg, Benson, and the others concluded that the man probably lighted the bulb by rubbing his hands to create static electricity.

In another instance, a Qigong master radiated his qi at both Benson and Eisenberg. Both admitted feeling vibrations, tingles, and warmth, but again they concluded that the effects were too subjective to merit acknowledging the existence of qi. The results would have to be repeated again and again, and those results would have to be studied under controlled conditions.

Near the middle of the book, Eisenberg cited what was for him the most compelling demonstration of qi. During a visit to a Beijing hospital, a doctor suspended a piece of paper from a string, then aimed his fingers at the paper, which slowly started to rotate. Apparently, Eisenberg was too flabbergasted to ask the Chinese doctor to repeat the demonstration, but in later encounters, he repeatedly asked the Qigong masters to perform similar feats to prove their skills.

Drs. Eisenberg and Benson didn't intend to cast doubt on Chinese Qigong. They were simply investigating a claim as best they knew how. And therein lies the problem: Qigong doesn't fit into the Western scientific paradigm. The mathematical language of science and its basic assumptions about proof are at odds with Qigong's insistence on cooperation, trust, and feeling. The scientific demand that results be repeatable also runs counter to the entropic reality of qi. Like earning a medical degree from Harvard, advanced Qigong is something that anyone can do *potentially,* yet in fact few people are disciplined enough. Just as a medical student has to sacrifice time and energy to complete the M.D., so too does the Qigong student have to work long and hard to perfect his or her Qigong. Unlike the Western medical doctor, however, the Qigong master doesn't work by abstraction, symbolic language, or even the physical act of surgery; the master works with "life force," and once that force is used up, it must be restored, which takes more work. To ask Qigong masters to repeat experimental results weakens them. If forced to submit to all the demands of Western science, a Qigong master's health might be threatened.

Still, Qigong masters who have been practicing since childhood step forward to take up the West's challenge. In September 1993, the *Washington Post* reported a demonstration by Cheng Wangpong to about three hundred scientists and doctors from the National Institutes of Health. Cheng shattered a rock without touching it. Predictably, NIH members expressed reserved surprise, insisting that more needed to be done to determine how the rock was shattered, but Cheng's demonstration may have greatly facilitated the West's efforts to prove qi exists. Among those who witnessed Cheng's feat was Roscoe O. Brady, chief of the developmental and metabolic branch of the National Institute of Neurological Disorders and Stroke. Brady, a world-famous research physician, was quoted as saying, "Maybe he has some ability to do this with electrophysiological energy, can synchronize it and harness [it]."

One of China's most famous Qigong masters, Dr. Yan Xin, has made many notable efforts to convince the Western world that Qigong is a force to be reckoned with. In 1987, while I was working at Beijing University, a series of fascinating experiments on Yan was conducted at nearby Qing Hua University, the M.I.T. of China. In one experiment (as reported in *Yan Xin and the Contemporary Sciences*), Yan radiated his qi and was able to denature radioactive isotopes from as far away as 2,000 kilometers. He also managed to bend a laser beam from the same distance. These are only a few of the staggering results Yan produced, which he managed to get published in English.

Though Yan has paved the way for future Western-style experiments, he may have inadvertently created a roadblock by insisting too strongly on the Chinese interpretation of Qigong. Yan is so advanced in Qigong that he can impart his qi to thousands by simply talking. As a result, many Chinese regard him with worshipful reverence. Out of a relative handful of patients whom he has healed instantly, the popular myth has risen that Yan, like Jesus, can restore vitality with a touch of his hand. Consequently, Yan has found himself a national superstar and the foremost spokesperson for Qigong. Some of his lectures to the Chinese have found their way into English translation, and Yan, who has visited the United States several times, now has an international Qigong association that is swiftly gaining membership. His lectures are distributed to all members, and the claims he makes in those lectures far exceed those made by the Qigong masters Eisenberg encountered. Yan argues that only by accepting certain fundamentals of Confucianism, Buddhism, and Taoism can a student hope to achieve notable success in Qigong. These tenets include filial devotion, humility, and absolute honesty, but Yan goes much further, making claims for Qigong that resemble some of the more extravagant claims of Indian yogis: telepathic and telekinetic powers, for example. Moreover, Yan asserts that some Qigong masters can live for hundreds of years or even longer. It's clear that Dr. Yan is one of the most powerful Qigong masters alive (Zhang, who was reluctant to endorse other Qigong masters, believes Yan to be one of the best), yet his revelations may, at least in the short-run, cause many Westerners to turn away from rather than toward Qigong.

Though no one in the West has satisfactorily proven the existence of qi, there exists a solid foundation for the notion that the human body is "energetic." Thermal photographs show that human bodies definitely radiate heat energy, and that variations in these radiations correspond to degrees of health. A vigorous, healthy person's thermal picture is far more vivid than that of a weak, unhealthy person. In addition, magnetic imaging resonance (MRI) machines provide pictures of the body's soft tissue, which cannot be shown with X rays. MRIs work by using a huge magnet to rotate in one direction the body's water molecules, which are held and then released. The movement of the molecules after release are then reconstructed through computer graphics to produce a picture. If there were no magnetic potential in the body, then MRI wouldn't work.

Western speculation about the electrodynamics of the human body and of disease has been around for a while. The theories of Bjorn Nordenstrom, a Swedish radiologist, provides a case in point. In the 1950s Nordenstrom proposed that the circulation of the blood creates a subtle electromagnetic field in the body. Armed with this theory, Nordenstrom has used electricity to successfully treat cancer patients. He inserts an electrode into the tumor and applies current. According to Nordenstrom, the electric charge creates an acid in the tumor's center. The acid then attracts white blood cells, which attack the tumor. Moreover, Nordenstrom's theory explains injuries in terms of electromagnetism. An injury to the body causes the injured site to experience a flux in voltage between positive and negative until a state of equilibrium is finally reached, a state Nordenstrom associates with healing. If this theory is generally true, then measuring electromagnetic fluctuations in various parts of the body might identify potential tumor sites.

Nordenstrom's theory and results notwithstanding, Western science remains entrenched in the attitude that energetics is an idea worthy only of speculation and research. A recent article in *Internal Strength*—a journal devoted to exploring "internal strength and qi"—reports that after ten years of study Dr. Robert Jahn, "a respected researcher in high-energy physics at Princeton," measured no significant electromagnetic energy in a large sampling of human subjects (though this study did not focus particularly on martial arts practitioners). He did, the article says, find that strong electromagnetic fields produced by machines have significant effect on human nervous tissue. The harmful effects of machine electromagnetism on humans is a topic I will return to in a later chapter. As for Dr. Jahn's failure to measure significant electromagnetic energy in humans, one wonders whether he would find marked differences if he were to compare his results with those obtained from deep-level Qigong practitioners.

It seems that Western science has been unable to prove the existence of qi largely because of conflicting cultural beliefs. There may be also a deep-seated, somewhat xenophobic, reflex at work in the West's resistance to the paradigms of thought from India and China: a fear that our externally focused Eurocentric culture is not the preeminent force destined to rule the world. I realize this speculation may strike some as wild or even offensive, yet it is based on repeated encounters with skeptical, even hostile members of my own culture. Science has replaced the church as the great bastion of truth and certitude in the West. It provides not only a means to economic and social ascension but also a source of comfort in an unruly world filled with uncertainties. Science compensates for having little to offer in the face of death by promising a life filled with explanations of causes and effects and with the sweet narcotic of being "right." As Korzybski observed, the human nervous system detests nothing more than the shock of the unexpected, and nothing leads to greater shocks than the unconscious assumption that the map *is* the territory. For this reason, the existing language of Western science may have to evolve before Qigong can be understood.

Until this evolution of understanding occurs, until qi can be measured and verified, Western science should concern itself with the more accessible manifestations of Qigong, such as the ability to enhance blood circulation, particularly along the path of the aorta. Such an apparent physiological phenomenon might be the starting place where the external-oriented technology of the West can do its best work. Once we understand that Qigong activates subtle aspects of the circulatory and immune systems, then we can compare its various methods to determine which is the most effective.

6

QIGONG THE CHINESE WAY

IF THE SEMANTICS OF WESTERN SCIENCE POSE A PROBLEM IN understanding Qigong, then so do the semantics of Chinese culture. The abundance of available English-language books on Chinese medicine, Qigong, and Taiji has helped spread important information, but most of these books are so entrenched in the Chinese paradigm that they prove daunting for most Westerners. Qigong books such as these do a slight disservice in that they blur the various levels of Qigong. In swimming, a dog-paddler and a freestylist are both *in the water,* but the similarities pretty much stop there. The same is true for Qigong practitioners of various levels.

Books that promote Chinese culture can be even more off-putting. Like their counterparts in the West, these champions of Chinese culture can be just as pedantic and infantile. They might insist that Qigong students not only learn all about Chinese medicine, but also become fluent in Chinese language, practice Chinese calligraphy, adopt Chinese manners, carry ceremonial swords, wear silk robes, and burn incense. Though some knowledge of Chinese medicine is necessary for learning Qigong, a successful deep-level student doesn't have to be fluent in ancient Chinese literature or proficient in acupuncture theory or herbology. Commitment to physical practice must come first.

It is essential, however, that one understand the paradigm that governs Chinese views on health. The Chinese model of nature and the human body is over four thousand years old, and it has produced a medical practice that rivals that of the West in the treatment of many diseases. For that reason alone, the Chinese paradigm merits consideration. Although there are existing books that go into far more detail, what is offered here is quite sufficient in terms of understanding deep-level Qigong. The portion of the model I deal with enriches the practice of Qigong and connects the mind more fully with the body. This is largely due to the high priority the Chinese model places on the body's organs and fluids. If students have the idea that what they feel during Qigong is the result of their internal organs, then they are automatically more grounded in the body than if they were thinking in terms of molecules and subatomic physics.

Also, at this point it is necessary that one take qi at face value. We are no longer playing by Western rules. In the Chinese model the concepts named exist a priori. A Westerner hoping to gain greater insight into Qigong must adapt to another set of laws, like the surface swimmer who finally gets up the nerve to hold his breath and plunge to the world below.

Humans and Nature: The Internal-External Connection

As I pointed out earlier, the Chinese paradigm begins with the tenet that human beings are microcosms of nature. To determine the inner workings of the human being, the Chinese go straight to the external world of nature. Ancient Taoists observed two important things about nature. First, everything in nature seems to function in opposition. The most pervasive of these opposites is darkness and light, represented by the yin/yang diagram, which stands for all dialectical processes in nature (dark/light, female/male, weak/strong, descending/ascending, curved/straight, death/life). Yin and yang are the primal driving forces of all natural phenomena. No matter how large or how small a phenomenon, it can always be broken down to a yin/yang dialectic. For example, a man, though predominately yang, also has a yin side. Likewise, a woman, though predominantly yin, has a yang side.

The second thing the Taoists saw in nature was an interplay between five elements—water, wood, fire, earth, and metal—all of which derive from yin and yang. These five elements interact according to two cycles: the *shen,* or "creative" cycle, and the *ke,* or "controlling" (sometimes translated as "destructive") cycle. In the control cycle, the elements have a linear relationship to one another that is more commonsensical than the creative cycle, which links the elements in a circle: water extinguishes fire; wood dominates earth; fire melts metal; earth contains water; and metal cuts wood. Though the circular creative cycle is a little less apparent, it was conceived on the basis of observing the five elements in nature. Water nourishes vegetation (wood), from which fire can be made by rubbing two sticks together. After the fire burns the wood, ash (or earth) is left behind. Metal lies beneath the surface of the earth, and metal condenses moisture on its surface, so that it appears to "create" water. Metal also turns liquid when heated to extreme temperatures. (This peculiar relation between water and metal made mercury a source of interest to ancient Taoists, who regarded the liquid metal as the external version of a similar substance in the body, called jing, which I'll explore in greater detail a bit later.)

Following out the deduction that outer nature reflects inner nature, the Taoists reasoned that the body represented a yin/yang dialectic and a recapitulation of the two five-element cycles. They concluded that the internal organs are the most important manifestations of yin/yang and the five elements, then observed further that the organs fall into two groups: the *zang* (solid) organs, and the *fu* (hollow) organs. The zang organs are yin; the fu organs are yang. Together they form the *zangfu,* and all health depends on its proper function, which obeys the laws of the five elements.

Though yin and yang are said to be of mutual importance, the yin or zang organs take top priority, as far as health is concerned. The yang or fu organs depend on the vitality of the zang organs for their fortitude. Therefore, if the zang organs can be strengthened, then the fu organs will follow suit. For this reason, fu organs are considered "companions" to the zang organs.

There are six major zang organs and their fu companions (in parentheses): the kidneys (bladder), the liver (gallbladder), the heart (small intes-

5 ELEMENTS

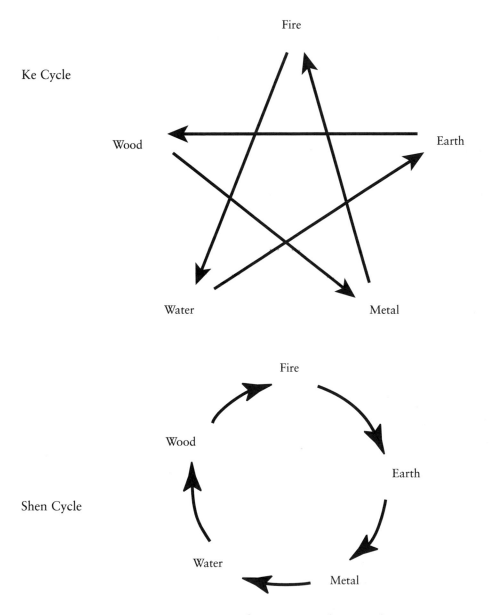

Ke Cycle

Fire

Wood

Earth

Water

Metal

Shen Cycle

Fire

Wood

Earth

Water

Metal

Figure 5. *The creative (shen) cycle and the controlling (ke) cycle of the Five Elements.*

THE ORGANS

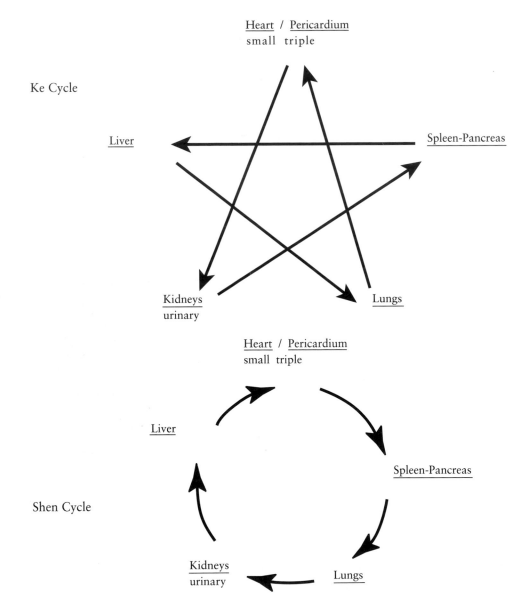

Figure 6. *The six organ systems follow the circular, creative (shen) and linear, controlling (ke) cycles of the Five Elements.*

tine), the pericardium ("triple heater," which has no Western anatomical counterpart), the spleen-pancreas (stomach), and the lungs (large intestine). Each organ represents one of the five elements. Kidney-bladder is water; liver-gallbladder is wood; heart–small intestine and pericardium–triple heater are fire; spleen-pancreas-stomach is earth; and lungs–large intestine is metal. These six organ systems follow the circular creative and the linear controlling cycles of the five elements.

The six organ systems also manage the movements and behavior of three basic fluids upon which all health depends: *jing,* or sexual fluid; *xue,* or blood, and *jin ye,* a broad term that encompasses the remaining fluids the body produces, such as lymph, saliva, sweat, tears, and gastrointestinal juices.

Finally, the six organ systems contain and manage the flow of qi, whose qualities reflect the particular element each organ represents. For example, the qi of the liver-gallbladder possesses the qualities of wood. In general, however, all the various elemental differences dissolve in the ocean of the body's qi, which exists a priori in the Chinese paradigm. Things move, the Chinese model holds, because qi makes them move. The verification of qi is that it can be *felt:* the electromagnetic sensation that is the hallmark of Qigong. If someone can't feel qi, the reason has more to do with deficiencies in that person and his or her practice than in the theory of qi.

Qi derives from three sources: the air, food sources, and the body itself. The lungs gather qi from the air. The spleen-pancreas extracts qi from food. And the kidneys, together with the other organs, store, circulate, and build the body's qi, which is inherited from the parents. Though air and food qi are important, the body's inherent qi or jing is the most important. Jing is both substance (yin) and energy (yang). In terms of substance, jing is sexual fluid. As energy, jing is the purest and most powerful form of qi the body possesses. Deep-level Qigong involves working with both the yin and yang of jing.

These three forms of qi move in and around the body through a complex series of *jing luo* (usually translated as "channels" or "meridians") or *mai* (translated as either "channels" or "pulses"). Acupuncture deals with all of the channels and the multitude of points (*xue wei*) along the channels. If the acupuncturist's entire map isn't already familiar, trying to absorb its plenteous nomenclature might be counterproductive to Qigong practice. The mind might be too preoccupied with verbal abstractions. The Qigong practitioner progresses by feeling. Analysis and memorization should be minimized, especially in the beginning. Qigong practitioners need know only a few details of the Chinese conceptual map while learning to "swim" and beginning to sense the field of qi that projects from the body and interacts with the surrounding air.

7

SENSING QI

WHEN I WAS LIVING IN BEIJING, I TOURED A BUDDHIST monastery one day and came upon a mural depicting an eye in the palm of Buddha. When I later spoke with Zhang about this peculiar depiction, he said the eye symbolized *lao gong,* an acupuncture point in the center of the palm. In Qigong practice, lao gong is far from a mere symbol. It literally becomes another eye, a sixth sense for discovering other important areas of the body's external qi field.

Although my first teacher had already helped me activate lao gong, Zhang's method was easier and produced better results. The first method I learned is a form of standing meditation known as "Iron Shirt" or Standing Post Qigong (figure 7), which entails keeping the legs slightly bent, the spine straight, and the arms held in an embracing gesture with the elbows lifted up. Zhang's Standing Post meditation is more comfortable. As in the Iron Shirt, the spine is erect, but the legs are kept straight without being taut. Most important, instead of lifting the elbows up, which causes muscles in the shoulders and neck to tighten, Zhang's method allows the elbows to relax downward toward the rib cage.

A   B

Figure 7. (A) *Iron-Shirt posture.* (B) *Zhang's standing-post posture.*

Swimming

During my first year of training with Zhang, we did very little talking during training. We talked afterward, always with the help of his wife or a student interpreter. This may seem a handicap, but because of my Western heritage our limited communication was an advantage. It forced me to concentrate on the physical moment, during which a lot of energetic inter-play occurred between us. I had to stay locked into Zhang's every move, gesture, and facial expression. I had to try to "read his mind," which assured a purity in our relationship. I was so concentrated on absorbing what he had to teach that I couldn't possibly think of much else. This kind of connection between student and teacher is what makes having a good teacher the best, if not the only, way to learn Qigong. Thought, action, and physical presence all work together, charging the common medium of the air, through which, I believe, qi transference occurs. My martial arts background gave me an advantage here. Imitation is the primary way that martial art is taught, so I was prepared for what to many might seem a frustrating way to learn.

After this one-on-one training, the next most important detail of Qigong practice is breathing, which stands to reason, since qi is commonly defined as air or breath. Zhang taught me a method known as reverse breathing, so called because the abdomen contracts instead of distends during inhalation. He taught me to breathe slowly and lightly through the nose, with the tongue curled up so that the tip rests comfortably against the upper palate. The slow, light breath minimizes the amount of oxygen the body uses, simulating the way animals breathe during hibernation. The curling of the tongue encourages breathing through the nose, which enhances the vascular and nervous systems of the sinus passages. The tongue is important for a number of other reasons: it is the liveliest organ in the mouth, and it is intimately connected to both the speech and taste centers of the brain and to digestion. Moreover, Chinese medicine proposes that the tongue is most closely related to the heart. Conjuncting this special organ with the conscious act of breathing, then, links in one behavior two profound aspects of the human organism.

In reverse breathing, the gentle contracting and relaxing of the lower abdominal muscles help draw the body's jing upward to mingle with the air qi in the lungs. Zhang warned me never to fill the lungs in the manner of aerobic exercise, and never to strongly contract the lower abdominal muscles. The contractions should be gentle and the breathing soft.

Next Zhang taught me a series of eight formal movements that had to be performed with the breathing. Six of these movements correlate to the six yin or zang organs; the other two movements correspond to the general yang or fu organs. Compared with learning Taiji or other forms of Chinese wushu, the Qigong movements were easy to learn. After a single class, I pretty much had them committed to memory.

In the next stage I practiced Zhang's more relaxed version of Standing Post Qigong. With eyes closed and arms held in a gentle embrace for five to seven minutes, I tried my best to focus on nothing but my reverse breathing. Then Zhang had me do an exercise called Tiger Plays with Ball (figure 8), in which the hands are held as though one were holding a beach ball between the palms. Slowly I began to rotate my hands in forward and backward circles, instantly provoking the sensation of electromagnetism

Figure 8. *Tiger Plays with Ball.*

radiating from one palm to the other, as though a sphere of charged air had formed between my hands.

After two to five minutes of "playing with the ball," Zhang had me lower my hands to my sides. They felt heavy and tingly. Then, on the inhale, Zhang brought his hands up over the top of his head, and I did the same, our left hands closest to our bodies because in Taoism yang or maleness accords with the left (women should have their right hands closest to their bodies). Then, on the exhale, we brought the hands down the front of our bodies until the lungs were empty and the hands were again resting by our sides. We repeated this process two more times. On the third time, we brought the hands to rest on the lower abdomen, just below the navel, where the body stores qi. This exercise is called Marrow Washing (figure 9, pages 50–51) because the hands push qi into the top of the skull, the contents of which were originally presumed to be a specialized form of bone marrow. Zhang simply referred to the exercise as "closing."

My first reaction to this exercise was that holding the arms up and then lowering them was a simple trick of circulation. The sensation of electromagnetism amounted to an illusion, created by first draining blood out of the hands then allowing it to return. If this were true, then the electromagnetic sensation would occur only during the exercise, which in time proves not to be the case. Once a person practices Qigong regularly for several months, the palms of the hands feel constantly magnetized. This sensation of lao gong having been brought to life is a prerequisite to deep-level Qigong practice.

After I had practiced this routine twice daily for a week, each time going through the closing motion, Zhang introduced the next phase: learning to sense *wai qi,* or "external energy," which surrounds the body in multiple orbits. This phase began with a normal session of the eight formal movements, followed by standing meditation, then a brief moment of Tiger Plays with Ball. Then Zhang lowered his hands in front of his lower abdomen. When I did the same, I was surprised to feel the same electromagnetic sensation. Next Zhang used his hands to describe a small circle in front of his waist. He kept circling his hands as he rotated to the left, then the right. As I followed along, the electromagnetic sensation continued. What I was feeling, Zhang said, was *dai mai* (figure 10), or the "belt pulse," an acupuncture channel that manifested externally as a hoop consisting of

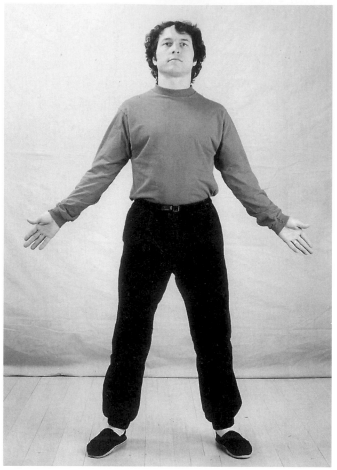

Figure 9. *Marrow Washing.*

A

three intersecting orbits of qi. These orbits encircle the waist in much the same way electron shells surround the nucleus of an atom (figure 10).

Zhang then used his hands to give dai mai a spin, much as someone might start a hula hoop, only in slow motion. Then, in the exact fashion of hula hooping, he moved the circle of qi by slowly rotating his hips. When I imitated him, I felt electromagnetism fluctuate as dai mai revolved with my waist rotation. After a few seconds, a noticeable submissiveness came over Zhang, as though he had stopped moving his hips and was instead letting his hips be moved by the slow-whirling, invisible circle. He then closed his eyes with a blissful smile, which I interpreted as an instruction not to think but to submit to the body's response to dai mai.

B   C

At first I found this difficult to do, but I was so surprised to actually feel dai mai that I followed Zhang's example. I came to see the routine as a vacillation between the conscious and unconscious minds. Though my conscious mind struggled to maintain itself by questioning, the unconscious asserted itself through feeling dai mai, which encouraged a pleasant relaxation. In moments when my conscious mind lost control, I felt fascinating subtleties in dai mai: circles within circles, traveling in opposite directions. Eventually I began to feel that all of the circles radiated out from tiny spirals made by my spine. I sensed that these spirals moved up and out, but I tried to stay focused on dai mai and the lower regions of the body, as Zhang seemed to imply.

I worked for over a week with dai mai, then Zhang moved me to the next step of the process. After I stood for five minutes with my arms in a gentle embrace, Zhang told me to exhale and bring my fingers close together without touching, then inhale and spread the hands apart. Next he rotated his hands as in Tiger Plays with Ball. I copied his movements, and immediately both arms felt thick with electromagnetism. Zhang moved his hands up to his face, then above his head, and I did the same, feeling

Figure 10. *Dai mai: the three orbitals surrounding the lower dan tian.*

changes in the electromagnetism as I went. Then Zhang lowered his hands to the embracing position and began circling his hands by moving his arms at the shoulder, a motion he called *tiao dong,* meaning "shoulder action," *tiao* referring to a long stick held across the shoulders, used for carrying pails of water. When I imitated him, I felt energy coursing around my upper torso.

What I was feeling this time, Zhang said, was *jian mai* (figure 11), or

Figure 11. *Jian mai: the three orbitals surrounding the middle dan tian.*

"shoulder pulse," another triumvirate of energy belts that mimics the atomic model. As with dai mai, I submitted to the compulsions of jian mai, rotating the shoulders about the upper spine. Then Zhang closed his eyes and began moving his hips according to the dai mai, and I did the same. As a result, my whole body felt encased in a moving mass of electromagnetism. When his arms got tired, Zhang lowered them and moved by dai mai. After they had recovered, he moved them up to feel jian mai. We moved like this for fifteen minutes.

At the end of the session, we closed in the usual fashion. Later Zhang explained that sensing dai mai and jian mai effectively connected the external qi of the lower and upper body. Because I had felt these qi belts for prolonged periods of time, my mind was beginning to believe they existed. Now my mind and my external qi were more closely united. I would, he said, never be the same.

Moving by dai mai and jian mai are examples of *zi fa dong,* or "automatic movements," a crucial aspect of successful deep-level Qigong. As far as I knew, dai mai and jian mai were the only forms of automatic movement there were. It would be a few more months before Zhang showed me I was wrong.

8

A U T O M A T I C
M O V E M E N T S
A N D   S I C K   Q I

ONE NIGHT IN LATE JANUARY, I RODE MY BIKE THROUGH
the cold windy gloom of Beijing University to a gymnasium where Zhang
was holding a special class he had invited me to attend. Walking the frigid,
empty corridors, I checked doors until I found the room, which was filled
with students standing stock-still, arms at sides, hands slightly lifted, eyes
barely open, as though on the verge of sleep. At the front of the room,
standing on top of an old table, Zhang signaled to me to find a spot and
follow along. I took up a position next to the door.

Slowly the collective, Taiji-like phase of Qigong began. I followed along,
contracting my abdomen on the inhale, relaxing it on the exhale, synchro-
nized to Zhang's soft-spoken commands, which sounded like singing. My
lower abdomen throbbed to life, the pulse rising up and spreading warmly
across my forehead before returning to the source. The Taiji-like movements came to an end, where I customarily stood in a gentle embracing
posture for about five minutes before moving according to dai mai and
jian mai. The Chinese students, however, were still moving, with odd gyrations and quiverings, arms flopping back and forth around their bodies,
hands smacking the lower back and lower abdomen, the motion slow and
regular at first, then speeding up to a frightful, chaotic pace. In no time
the entire room became filled with flailing, staggering people, spontaneous

groans, shouts, and wails erupting like fireworks. Some students stood in place and pounded themselves. Others hopped around like children throwing tantrums. A few began doing what appeared to be wushu maneuvers. One woman pranced across the room and tossed imaginary flowers as she went, an odd smile on her face. Within minutes several students were in tears, and, as though summoned, the more placid students gravitated toward the stricken ones, who let the hands of comforting companions wave up and down their bodies without touching. Suddenly a mass of students were mowed down by a small young man who had turned himself into a human cannonball. He rolled head over heels across the floor, then began scooting on his hindquarters like a dog wiping itself on the grass. The holy-rolling of American charismatic churches seemed tame by comparison.

In the midst of this human storm, Zhang moved placidly, hands outstretched and waving, radiating qi, I supposed. Every now and then, Zhang paused beside a student and skimmed his hands around the student's head. As a final gesture Zhang always moved his hands down toward the student's lower abdomen, whereupon he moved to the next person. Zhang spent a long while near one young woman who was spinning around and around as though she were caught in a relentless, invisible vortex. Zhang spoke gently to her, and she responded each time by shaking her head no, then spinning once more out of control. Zhang held out his hand until she stopped spinning. Her knees buckled and she fell softly to the floor. Zhang stood over her and moved his hands from the top of her head to her feet. Then he pulled her onto her right side and tucked her knees into her chest for her, a position Zhang called the Reclining Buddha—a method of resting he recommended for people too exhausted to meditate sitting upright.

After about fifteen minutes of continous fury, Zhang softly summoned everyone to stillness. The students on the floor stood and, together with everyone else, opened their eyes and went through the closing motion three times, concluding by placing both hands across the lower abdomen. Then we all sat in the half-lotus position for meditation.

I was simply confused, and my meditation was unstable as a result. My thoughts wandered all over the place, swirling generally around the notion that I had just been exposed to mass lunacy. When the meditation ended, Zhang led the class through a series of massages that covered the entire body, beginning with the eyes, ranging down to the feet and hands, concluding with the heart. Zhang gave a final piece of advice, which I couldn't understand; then the students filed out of the room.

Zhang came over to me and said, "What do you think?"

"Interesting," I responded, lacking the words to say that I was both confused and disturbed by what I had seen.

Zhang smacked my shoulder and asked, "Are you afraid of these movements?"

I laughed and said no, but in retrospect I can say that I *was* afraid in a sense—afraid of looking foolish. I told Zhang that I was happy with what he had taught me and I didn't feel a need to go any further. He gave me an odd smile that suggested, "Wrong answer."

A few days later Zhang came to my room and with a smiling, robust face told me that I would have to move as the Chinese students had moved because I had "a lot of sick qi" in my body. The word *sick* stung like a wasp. When I asked Zhang what he meant, he answered that healthy qi moved like water, but sick qi didn't move. Zhang told me to "cast away sick qi," flicking his hands as though trying to shake off some slimy, sticky substance. Then he pointed at my abdomen and said that my zangfu was filled with sick qi and that the only way to get rid of it was to shake as the Chinese students had done.

At this point my wrist was still hurting, and I was terrified of making it worse. But I felt I had more to gain by trying Zhang's method. After all, he had already given me the ability to fight off common ailments. So I agreed, somewhat timidly.

Zhang showed me two general movements that come naturally. The first involves pivoting at the waist so that the arms swing around and strike the lower abdomen in front and a parallel spot on the lower back; then, as the pivoting continues, the arms travel up both the front and the back of the body (figure 12, pages 58–59). The hands striking the body open various channels and allow qi to flow more smoothly. They also combine with the pelvic gyrations to churn both blood and fluids throughout the entire zangfu. The second general movement is the same sort of

Figure 12. *The "automatic movements" of pivoting and striking.*

A

bouncing motion toddlers do instinctively, seeming to derive great pleasure from it. It was softer and more comforting than the first, but it too churned the body's juices along with the qi contained in those juices.

Even better, Zhang said, was a combination of the two movements, the body gyrating and bouncing at the same time, like a washing machine, the arms flailing and striking the front and back repeatedly. But there was an even more effective movement, one that people "feared" because it was painful, but if I wanted to get rid of sick qi, I would have to do it: a veritable fit, shaking the body violently from the waist, the arms forced out to the sides like Elvis Presley reaching the final note in a gut-wrenching song.

B

C

After these demonstrations, all of which struck me as absurd, Zhang led me through the Taiji-like movements, and after a few minutes, he dropped his hands and swayed gently. I imitated him. Then I forced the swaying into harder motion. I let my arms flop, striking the lower abdomen and lower back. I let my mind go, diffusing inhibitory thoughts by reminding myself that my body was full of sick qi that needed to be "cast away," as Zhang had put it. My movements became harder, my hands striking higher on my body, pounding into the areas housing the kidneys, liver, spleen, heart, and lungs. The blows stung, but I still didn't feel anything internally. I added the bouncing movement to the gyrations, and immediately a thick ache seized my right kidney and radiated into the liver. "It's just a cramp," I told myself, but the ache was irritating, and I moved harder, finally breaking into the berserk flapping which my students and I now fondly refer to as "the Elvis."

The ache focused sharply, like a knife wound, and it traveled from the liver up into my right shoulder, then moved down my right arm to my wrist. The pain swelled so greatly that I cried out, and I had no thought except driving the sensation out of my body. Slowly the thick cramp diminished in my kidney, then liver, then right shoulder, seeming to flow down and off my right arm. The cramp remained, but it had definitely lessened, and I became even more determined to drive it from my body. Still the pain lingered, and exhaustion finally prevailed. I collapsed in a spastic, stricken heap, gasping and clawing the floor of my room. After lying flat on my back for a few minutes, I sensed Zhang standing over me, hands waving up and down my body. A burning warmth developed over my heart, then it moved to my liver, where the pain seemed to concentrate, and then moved down and out my right leg.

As Zhang pulled me to my feet, the pain continued to radiate mildly, though it quickly receded inside my organs. I followed Zhang's movements, waving the hands up and down the front of the body, herding agitated qi down to the lower abdomen for storage.

In the weeks that followed, I continued such hard automatic movements whenever I practiced. The movements were painful every time, but the pain increasingly diminished. When doing "the Elvis" no longer caused the cramping sensation in my right kidney and liver, the pain in my wrist simultaneously vanished. According to Zhang, my wrist hadn't healed because of a qi block residing deep inside my right kidney and liver. The hard movements had driven the sick qi from deep within to the surface, where I was able to literally shake it off.

Hard automatic movements such as these may seem ridiculous and even dangerous to Westerners, but they are a big part of what can make Qigong such an effective healing method. It took a lot of practice and a lot of hands-on experience before I came to understand the nature of these automatic movements and their importance in combating sick qi, the root cause of all disease.

The more violent quivering action is called *dou dong* (literally "shaking movement"), an indication of qi imbalances in the zangfu. This imbalance begins with the stagnation of jing, the flow of which rules qi and the other bodily fluids. Jing can stagnate because of either bad jing inherited from parents or a variety of behaviors, both of which I'll discuss later. Once jing stops working properly, the streams of qi coursing in and across the body slow and eventually clog. Next, the blood, which follows qi in a symbiotic fashion, slows. Then, jin ye, the body's collective fluid, slows. Finally the tissues themselves atrophy, a sign which even Western medicine regards as pathological: this occurs, for example, in patients with cirrhosis of the liver or malignant growths, both of which are hard relative to benign growths, which tend to be soft.

By moving hard, an individual can sense these imbalances, which feel superficially like knots of energy, more profoundly like muscular kinks and cramps: blockages, in other words. Violent movement exposes the deep location of these blockages, which are really stagnant qi. This stagnation develops over time into substantive knots of tissue in the organs themselves, where the lack of nerves makes sensation impossible. Automatic movement, which begins quietly on its own, is the language of kinesis, describing the body's pathology. The more serious the imbalance, the more crazy the motion. In order to make the movements curative, the will has to be enlisted, as in the case of dai mai and jian mai, a dance between conscious and unconscious faculties. The object is to move until the knots become painful, then to keep moving until either the knots dissolve or the individual collapses, at which point the teacher moves in and uses qi to disperse the knots. In a large class such as the one I witnessed, Zhang had to be selective. He later told me that many students simply pretended to move wildly to get more attention. For this reason Zhang usually focused on one or two people at a time. Though he was able to infuse only a relatively small number at a given time, there were always special honest and sincere people who, he claimed, drew in his qi without his having to focus on them directly.

When the harder movements become intolerably painful, the conscious mind resists, at which point the slower automatic movements of dai mai and jian mai take over, working their slow magic on the knots the way water erodes stone. Over time, if the pathology has not progressed to the point of substantive manifestation, such as a malignant tumor, then Qigong can prevail over the blockage. In some cases, even when pathology has progressed to the point of cancer, the teacher can help the student dissolve the malignancy.

9

QI
AND
RESISTANCE

As crazy as automatic movements seem, their aerobic benefit is easy to see. Prolonged shaking and bouncing, like trampolining and aerobic dancing, increase respiration, raise the heart rate, and stimulate the lymphatic system. Automatic movements and aerobics differ, however, in a number of ways. First, the aerobic exerciser tries to avoid getting "cramps," defined as an excess of lactic acid in the muscle. The automatic mover tries to get cramps in order to locate stagnant qi. Second, the aerobic exerciser is always in control. The automatic mover remains in a semiconscious state and strives to lose control so that the Qigong master can inject qi into the body. Third, since aerobic exercise requires a lot of physical stress and strain, it helps develop discipline and willpower. By contrast, the automatic movements of Qigong break down will and resistance so that the individual is able to become more submissive, permitting the master's qi to enter the body with less obstruction.

This last difference bears more detailed scrutiny. Aerobic exercise is not premised on the intimate and profound connection between states of mind and of body. By aerobic standards, a person can have a perfectly healthy body and an unhealthy mind. By Qigong standards, both mind and body must be healthy. In fact, every aspect of physical reality, both mental and physical, is subject to the laws of qi flow. Emotion is the subjective experience of qi, moving or stagnant or somewhere in between. The cause of mental illness is the same as that of physical illness: stagnant qi. Likewise, the remedy is the same: enhance the flow of qi.

In the West, psychotherapists treating mental illness struggle against "resistance" in their clients; when the resistance is released, the client can move toward mental health. The Qigong master has a similar problem, but in China the Confucian tradition of deference to the teacher takes care of most of this resistance. In the West, the Qigong teacher's job is far more complicated and difficult. The teacher cannot expect the same degree of cooperation from Western students, who tend to be far more resistant than their Asian counterparts. It is in the nature of the Western paradigm for people to be independent-minded. In this regard, the automatic movements can be a valuable ally. In automatic movement, students break down their own resistance through experiencing self-inflicted discomfort and exhaustion. If a student collapses after moving hard for a long period of time (eight to ten minutes), mind, body, and qi are in a state of openness and rarefaction.

This doesn't mean that Qigong is a permanent cure for mental illness. Regression can and will occur without regular practice. Zhang told me that of the millions of Chinese who practice Qigong, only a relative handful ever experiences the pulse in the lower abdomen, and even fewer can make their qi travel in their bodies. They need to be as close as possible to a Qigong master in order for a transfusion of qi to occur. With so many people in a class, such a transfusion between master and student is difficult and thinly spread. A student might temporarily feel the lower abdomen come to life, only to have the feeling vanish in a matter of weeks under the tyranny of old patterns that refused to change. This, Zhang said, was evidence of a "resistant mind," which relishes habit, familiarity, and comfort.

Wushu

Though most people regard it as a form of either self-defense or martial ballet, wushu also offers an alternate way of coaxing qi flow. Learning wushu is like learning choreographed dance or ballet. For the more strenu-

A

B

Figure 13. *The first-pattern movements, which promote the fu organs:* (A) *"Breaststroke,"* (B) *Yang-Style Reinforced Push, and* (C) *Changquan Double-Hand Push.*

C

A

B

Figure 14. *The second-pattern movements, which promote the fu organs:* (A) *"Butterfly Stroke,"* (B) *Yang-Style Taiji Box the Ears, and* (C) *Changquan Reinforced Punch.*

C

A

B

Figure 15. *Movements that promote the liver:*
(A) *Forward Circle, right;*
(B) *Opening of Chen-Style Taiji;*
 and (C) *Pigua Palm-Strike, right.*

C

A

B

Figure 16. *Movements that promote the spleen-pancreas: (A) Forward Circle, left; (B) Bagua Twist to the Left; (C) Pigua Palm Strike, left.*

C

ous external forms, the student must be limber and have strong muscles. Though the forms themselves enhance flexibility and strength, the student should undergo a series of stretches and muscle-building exercises in conjunction with practicing the forms. As for internal wushu such as Taiji, the need for preliminary exercise is less necessary. Internal wushu is actually a form of Qigong with the explicit purpose of building qi for self-defense. If the internalist's qi is strong, he or she can both withstand blows and strike with extraordinary power.

Figure 17. *Movements that promote the heart and pericardium:*
(A) Catch and Release, (B) *Chen-Style Taiji Part the Wild Horse's Mane,*
(C) Bajiquan Punch, and (D) *Changquan Side Punch.*

A   B

As I pointed out earlier, many motions and postures of internal wushu, especially Taijiquan, relate directly to Qigong movements. These Taiji-like Qigong movements stimulate the zangfu. The following is a brief catalogue of these movements according to the particular organs they help stimulate.

Movements that involve both arms projecting forward from the abdomen activate the fu or digestive organs. The arms may project from the abdomen in two ways: either with the arms close together as they move forward, or with the arms spreading outward during the forward motion and narrowing at the farthest point of extension. The first of these two patterns appears in Yang-style Taiji (the most popular form of Taijiquan) as a reinforced push, which keeps the arms together instead of spread apart (figure 13). A similar movement with the arms projecting from the

C

D

A   B   C

Figure 18. *Movements that promote the lungs:* (A) *Stoop,* (B) *Stand,*
(C) *Yang-Style Taiji Kick,* (D) *Bagua Single-Leg Standing Finger Strike,*
and (E) *Changquan Slap-Kick.*

sides is recapitulated more rigidly in the external style of Changquan (Long Fist). The second pattern shows up again in the Yang style with a movement called Box the Ears. A similar posture can be found in Changquan (figure 14).

In contrast to the fu organs, the zang organs receive more particular treatment in the movements of internal and external wushu. In Zhang's version, the movement that enhances the liver is a coiling action to the right, the side where the liver is located. This coiling action is recapitulated in the opening movement of Chen-style Taiji, the oldest and most advanced form of Taijiquan. In the case of an external form of wushu called *pigua,* the same rightward movement is taken to an extreme, where coiling at the waist wraps the practitioner's arms around the body (figure 15).

Just as the right side is the locus of the liver, so is the left the locus of

D   E

the spleen-pancreas, and in keeping with this symmetry, movements that stimulate the spleen-pancreas coil to the left (figure 16).

The posture for the heart and pericardium occurs in Chen-style Taijiquan, as well as in another internal style, called Bajiquan (Eight Extremities Fist). In Changquan, the same posture is lengthened and tightened (figure 17).

Movements that stimulate the lungs involve raising the arms to the sides or above the head. Zhang's Qigong combines such movements with a stooping action, which effectively turns the body into a bellows, squeezing air out of the lungs as the stooping takes place. Such an action also puts pressure on the kidneys, where the body's jing is housed, so that in addition to pumping out air, stooping milks jing from the kidneys. In wushu as well as in Zhang's Qigong, standing movements usually follow stooping movements, which not only alleviates pressure on the lungs and kidneys, but also allows liberated jing to enter the body's qi circulatory system. To prolong the milking effect of the stoop, the standing part of Zhang's Qigong movements involves lifting one leg in the manner of a crane so that

71

A

Figure 19. *Movements that promote the kidneys:*
(A) Yang-Style Snake Creeps Down, (B) Golden Cock
Stands on One Leg, (C) Changquan Floor Strike,
and (D) Changquan Standing Posture.

B

C

D

pressure on the kidneys continues. This same action recurs in the Yang-style Taiji heel kick, *Bagua Zhang* (Eight Diagrams Palm), and in a general kicking exercise for Changquan (figure 18).

Though these movements correspond in general to individual organs, Zhang was careful to emphasize that no movement had a singular, isolated effect on a specific organ. Because nature compels particular organs to interdepend through the shen and ke cycles, each movement ultimately affects the entire zangfu. But vitality, or the cultivation thereof, must begin somewhere, and as far as the Chinese paradigm is concerned, the kidneys are it. If the kidneys' qi equals the body's jing, then all health depends on the strength or weakness of kidney qi. By this logic, Qigong and internal wushu (especially Taijiquan) focuses attention on preserving and developing the kidneys.

If stooping and single-leg standing postures stimulate kidney qi, then the Taiji movements known as Snake Creeps Down and Golden Cock Stands on One Leg thoroughly work the kidney meridian in the leg. Similarly, Changquan uses similar postures, though in it, unlike Taiji, the muscles are contracted and motion occurs swiftly. The ability to perform these strenuous moves with grace and proper posture is a good indication of the overall strength of the kidney system (figure 19).

To understand how these movements relate to the kidneys, we can refer again to the Chinese medical model. The kidneys, like all of the body's organs, are considered by Chinese medicine to be more than lumps of flesh in the midst of our bodies. They are also energies that loop and coil along channels that flow like rivers in and around our bodies. The acupuncture kidney channel flows from the bottom of the foot and up the inside of the leg almost to the genital region, where the channel then moves inside the body to flow up toward and terminate at the root of the tongue. A branch springs from the chest and flows along the surface of the body, from lower abdomen to collarbone (figure 20).

From this representation we can see that the legs play a vital role in the circulation of kidney qi. In fact, Zhang claimed that a general assessment of qi and health can be made from observing the legs of an individual. The legs are like the roots of trees that draw up nourishment from the ground. When people age, their legs shrivel. When athletes lose strength, their knees and ankles fail. In fact the area from the navel and the lower back

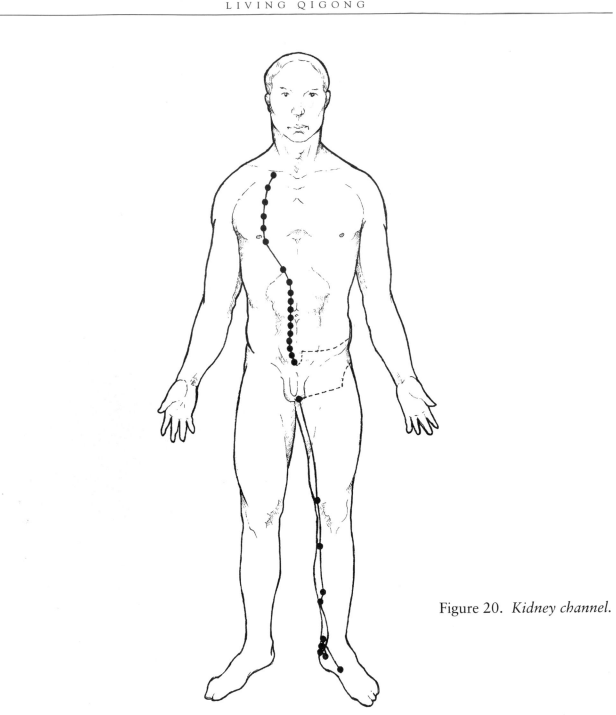

Figure 20. *Kidney channel.*

down to the toes reveals the yin conditions of the body. The upper body, which had always been my focus in defining strength or beauty, indicates yang conditions. Without a healthy yin base, the yang rots. When I asked Zhang when I would be able to teach Qigong, he said that I would first have to execute with my legs three consecutive sweeps that draw three perfect interlocking circles on the ground. Then I would be ready.

To activate kidney qi, however, practitioners need not force themselves into a full split or any such demanding posture. The Qigong movement that corresponds most directly to the kidneys involves vertically raising and lowering the arms while concomitantly straightening and bending the knees, then on a horizontal plane separating and bringing together the hands, as though playing an accordian, while the knees simultaneously straighten and bend. These simple, gentle movements are the basis of Yang-style Taiji, the general motion of which consists of raising, lowering, separating, and bringing together the hands. Such movements energize lao gong in the center of the palm, permitting the practitioner to begin sensing the interplay between the body's electrochemistry and the surrounding air, the outermost layer of kidney qi (figure 21).

If any exercise that strengthens the legs builds kidney qi and enhances health, then running, playing tennis, and even weight lifting—all of which build the legs—enhance kidney qi. But wushu does far more than build the legs. Because many of its postures resemble those of Qigong, wushu is more complete than most exercises. In addition to using muscles, the motions of wushu routines stimulate the qi residing in the zangfu. Zhang referred to using wushu in conjunction with Qigong as *wushugong,* and a session typically consisted of preliminary stretches, followed by an aerobically challenging Changquan routine. After regaining our breath by walking in circles and collecting our qi with our hands, we then turned to a less aerobic, internal form such as Bajiquan, which is slower than Changquan but faster than Taijiquan, the last form practiced in the session. We concluded by going into gentle automatic movements, settling finally on the ground for meditation. The wushu routines generally took about twenty or thirty minutes, the meditation about the same amount of time.

I should mention at this point that both hard automatic movements and wushu should be performed in the presence of a qualified teacher. While there is less cause for worry with automatic movements, injuries can occur

A   B   C

Figure 21. *Movements that promote the kidneys:* (A) Up, (B) Down,
(C) Separate, (D) Together, (E) Transition, and (F) Yang-Style Taiji Part
the Wild Horse's Mane.

D   E   F

in each case. A good teacher, however, can show students how to avoid injury. As for what constitutes a good teacher, I wish to make a distinction here between wushu and Qigong. To learn physical movements from someone is one thing, but to receive someone's qi is quite different. For this reason, I define a good teacher as one who either can demonstrate the lower abdominal pulse in various parts of his or her body or can project qi from the hands so that it can be felt strongly. Given the Western tendency toward resistance and skepticism, the latter part of the definition is less reliable. Thus, I strongly recommend the lower abdominal pulse and the ability to move it as a basic criterion for determining "internal" ability. And a crucial aspect of cultivating that ability can be found in meditation.

10

QIGONG MEDITATION AND YOGA

Iᴆ ᴛʜᴇ ᴍᴏᴠɪɴɢ ᴀsᴘᴇᴄᴛ ᴏғ Qɪɢᴏɴɢ ɪs ᴀɴᴀʟᴏɢᴏᴜs ᴛᴏ sᴡɪᴍ-ming along the surface of a body of water, then meditation resembles submersion. Swimming underwater requires an entirely different set of skills than does surface swimming; the same is true of *dong gong* (moving Qigong) and *jing gong* (motionless Qigong). Though motionless Qigong may be performed standing, the body may tend to move automatically the more relaxed the person becomes. Sitting on the floor or in a chair reduces this tendency and allows the practitioner to focus more on the body's trunk, where the most important qi resides. If sitting on the floor, the practitioner may cross the legs "Indian-style," half-lotus, or full-lotus (see figure 46 on page 158). If the practitioner is unable to sit on the floor, he or she should sit near the front edge of a chair, with the back away from the backrest of the chair. In both cases, the back should be straight without being rigid, and the head should be held up, as though it were being pulled slightly upward by a thin wire "extending to heaven."

The lotus posture is the same as that prescribed in Hindu yoga and Buddhist meditation, both of which, like Qigong, champion practice over theory. Both yoga and Buddhist meditation contend that a line of spiritual energy runs from the groin up the front of the body to the middle of the forehead, the most significant point in both cosmologies. When they get into the particulars of this spiritual line, however, the Hindu and the Buddhist part company. Hindu yoga identifies seven chakras, or energy centers, along the line, located at the anus, genitals, navel, heart, throat, forehead, and crown (figure 22). In the first few hundred years after its founding, Buddhist meditation didn't rely on chakras but eventually came to acknowledge four energy centers at the navel, heart, throat, and crown.

By the twelfth century, Muslim invaders had all but crushed Buddhism in India, but the religion had already migrated across the Himalayas into Tibet, where its practices took root and evolved. When the Mongols conquered both China and Tibet, they helped spread Tibetan Buddhism throughout China, and Buddhism underwent more changes, mingling with Taoism and Confucianism. From the confluence of Taoism, Buddhism, and Confucianism, Zhang's form of Qigong sprang. Zhang can trace his Qigong legacy back as far as three hundred years, though it appeared perhaps five hundred years ago. According to Zhang, the image of the red line rising and falling with the breath is a Buddhist practice derived from Hindu meditation.

The broad purpose of both Hindu yoga and Buddhist meditation is to dissolve attachment to this life by achieving a higher state of consciousness wherein the ego itself dissipates. Though Zhang never used these exact words to describe the aim of his Qigong meditation, he pointed, literally, in that direction one night when I asked him to explain the purpose of Qigong meditation. This happened shortly before I experienced the lower abdominal pulse, so I was still using Zhi Xiaomeng as an interpreter. The three of us were sitting on the floor of my room. Zhang traced with his finger on the carpet an inverted triangle and pointed at the apex, saying, "This is us." Then he pointed to the upside-down base of the triangle and began talking. Zhi said, "The teacher says that when we first begin meditating, our thoughts are like the base of the triangle."

With his pointed finger Zhang divided the triangle's base and began naming each part.

"We think about what we have to do during the day," said Zhi. "We think about what we have to do tomorrow. We think about what someone said to us long ago, and we think about what we wish we had said back to them."

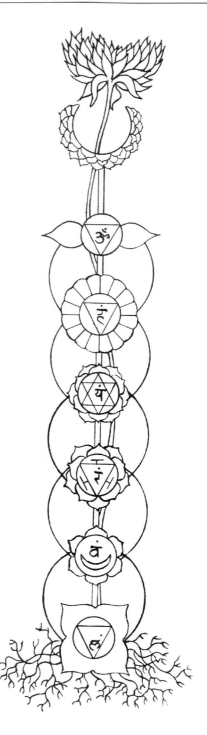

Figure 22. *The Hindu chakra line.*

Zhang created with his finger another base, farther down the sides, so that the triangle grew smaller.

"Later," Zhi said, "we think less about the past, only about things that bother us now and in the future."

Zhang brought the base down the sides even farther.

"And later we think even less about those things."

Zhang touched the apex of the triangle, perched over the head of the archetypal meditator.

"Finally we think about nothing at all." Zhi looked directly into my face. "Then he says we become 'very smart.'"

At the time I didn't understand what Zhang was talking about, but gradually I started to get the idea. Only by being silent and motionless can the student find the hidden power of the body.

Kriya, Dan Tian, and the Three Emperors

Though Hindu yoga takes many forms and has a number of purposes, the form known as kriya, touted by Paramahansa Yogananda as the supreme form toward which all other yogas build, closely resembles Qigong in its basic somatic cosmology. Put simply, the science of kriya holds that all humans possess divine energy stored in the lower part of the body. This energy is described as a primal breath, distinguished from the breath accomplished through the lungs. The purpose of kriya meditation is to bring this primal breath, or prana, up the spine to the higher chakras. As this energy rises, the yogi builds the "astral body," the yogi's energetic corpus for the next life. The yogi also achieves greater spiritual health by ridding him- or herself of "bad karma," sins accumulated from former existences. Upon reaching a certain level of competency, a kriya yoga master can eliminate bad karma through meditation. This sounds good, but each member of the vast majority has millions and millions of years of bad karma to his or her credit, so unless the individual meditates for approximately eight hours of every day throughout a lifetime, a tremendous amount of bad karma remains.

Like the kriya yoga concept of prana, Taoist Qigong posits jing, the purest form of qi, as its version of the primal breath. Moreover, the object of Qigong is to move this primal breath from the lower part of the body to the higher parts. This lower part of the body is called the *dan tian,* located just below the navel, where the body's most precious qi resides. There are actually three dan tians, corresponding to three of the chakras: navel, heart, and forehead (figure 23). Of the three, the lower dan tian is the most basic, a necessary condition for the development of the other two.

The literal translation of *dan tian* is "red field," though some translate

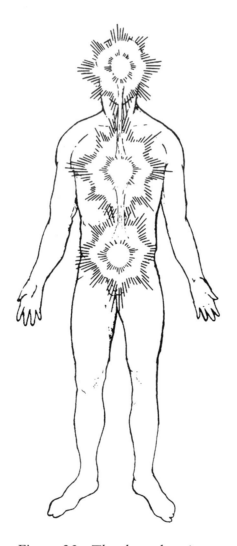

Figure 23. *The three dan tians.*

82

it as "field of the elixir." The term generally refers to the lower dan tian, from which qi supposedly issues, circulates throughout the body, then returns. Thus the word *field*—as in "field of wheat"—is appropriate. A field generates life, which then perishes and returns to the ground. The words *red* and *elixir,* however, require more explanation. Ancient Taoists were fascinated with cinnabar, or red mercury—its metallic and liquid properties, as well as its lively responses to temperature. Cinnabar became a natural correlative to the body's jing, which, perhaps by association, came to be seen as a "red elixir" that can be cultivated inside the body. It is no small coincidence that Hindu yoga connects the color red with the navel chakra.

Zhang's Qigong goes by the formal name San Huang Menpai Gong, literally "The Three Emperors School of Hard-earned Skill." *Gong* is an abbreviation for both *gongfu* (a synonym for martial art) and *qigong*. The "Three Emperors" are the three dan tians, which, in keeping with the Taoist focus on nature, correspond to three primal forces of nature: heaven, human being, and earth. The upper dan tian represents heaven; the middle, human being; and the lower, appropriately, the earth.

This cosmology seems a neat package, but for a Westerner it raises more questions than it answers. When Zhang first taught me about it, I had to know just what this dan tian thing *was,* so one night I visited Zhang and his family to ask him more about it. Zhang explained, with Liu Ziping translating, that when a baby is born, there is only dan tian. While the baby is still inside the mother, dan tian grows to become the zangfu. Zhang held up one finger and said, "*Shen,*" the kidneys, the water element. Then Zhang laid his hand over his left pectoral and said, "*Xin,*" the heart, the fire element. I assumed he was telling me that an embryo formed kidneys first, then a heart, which contradicts the fact that the heart forms a week or more before the primitive kidneys. But I gathered through further discussion that Zhang was saying that the prototype for the most important organs for health—first the kidneys, then the heart—initially resides in dan tian. In fact, the first location of the embryo's primitive heart is in the lower abdomen.

Next Zhang drew across his abdomen with his finger imaginary lines leading to all his zangfu. As he talked, Liu translated that the spine is like a tree from which all of the body's organs, including the brain, spring.

"What happens when we die?" I asked abruptly.

Liu Ziping spoke with her husband, then gave the answer: "When we sit, we are already dead."

I blinked at Zhang, who smiled, skin glowing healthily. I could follow this logic. If death was the cessation of moving life, then sitting still was a sort of calculus of death.

"But where does he think we go after death?" I asked.

Zhang and Liu exchanged words, then she said, "He says that if we practice Qigong, after death our skin, hair, and bones will pass away, but dan tian will still remain."

This was without a doubt the most staggering revelation Zhang made during my two years of training with him. He seemed to be equating dan tian with the "soul." If this were true, then Qigong was far more than a mere health exercise for the body. Perhaps it literally released and cultivated the soul in the body. I remember looking at my injured wrist and imagining the stratification of marrow, bone, muscles, tendons, vessels, and blood, coursing every second, carrying particles whose chemical complexity might never be fathomed. Was it so far-fetched to acknowledge that these strata faded into one another, like the colors of the spectrum, that *Gray's Anatomy,* a product of eighteenth-century thinking, had it wrong? Could the body be atomized and partitioned—marrow separate from bone, bone separate from muscle, muscle separate from skin, skin separate from blood—and still be fully appreciated? I flexed my fingers, the vessels in the forearm swelling, muscles moving smoothly with even the slightest bend of a digit. I imagined each layer of the body dying away, leaving only bone, which finally would decay and leave only a faint lambency, a sliver of the soul, which would retreat to its source in dan tian.

After that night I could no longer think of the dan tian as merely an obscure physiological process. The work done with Qigong, like that done with kriya yoga, may project beyond this life, into the next. In this way, the sensation of you haizi, or lower abdominal pulse, its curative ascent to the head, the emanation of qi from the hands, and the bands of qi swirling around the waist and shoulders may well parallel what Hindus mean by the "astral body" and what Christians call the soul.

11

THE THREE LEVELS
OF QIGONG

Ren Mai

The first step in the first level of deep Qigong practice involves the rising and falling of the pulse of the lower dan tian up and down through the other two dan tians. In my case, the pulse rose up quite soon after I started Qigong practice, but this isn't the case for everyone. The reason why this sometimes takes time to develop can be explained in terms of Taoism and Chinese medicine. According to contemporary Chinese medicine, *ren mai*—the conception, or pulse, channel—contains twenty-four acupuncture points. The main function of the ren mai is to connect and nourish the three dan tians. The complete opening of ren mai is essential to achieving the full benefits of Qigong. The automatic movements of Qigong practice sometimes help open ren mai for meditation practice, but more often than not ren mai fails to open because the mind is too busy, preoccupied with everyday or past difficulties, or simply too resistant, filled with the unconscious skepticism that is part of the legacy of Western culture. I lacked a good deal of this skepticism, which probably accounted for my quick response. But I also lacked the mental discipline to clear my mind, which resulted in inconsistent Qigong experiences. By focusing on the rise and fall of the pulse, the practitioner approaches *becoming* the pulse, and thoughts diminish accordingly.

Once ren mai opens and thinking becomes less chaotic, the student enters more deeply into Qigong. Practicing with ren mai helps do two important things: it develops the lower dan tian, and it helps rid the body of sick qi. The rise and fall of qi on ren mai builds and enlarges dan tian the way lifting weights builds and enlarges a bicep. Moreover, healthy qi rising to the upper dan tian disrupts pockets of sick qi hiding in the trunk and head of the body and pushes the sick qi from pores and facial orifices. When this happens, the student's skin, eyes, ears, and scalp itch and feel prickly, as though tiny ants were crawling over the surface of the body. Though these experiences may seem unpleasant, they are a necessary phase in gaining control of health.

The pathway of ren mai runs along the body's surface (figure 24A), which allows for the expulsion of sick qi. Occasionally, however, the practitioner may feel the pulse on a deeper level along the same general pathway. In such cases qi rises by means of *chong mai,* an internal channel that aids ren mai in its cleansing function (figure 24B). At the first level of deep Qigong practice, sensing the pulse along chong mai will most likely come and go, from time to time creating an elongated circular pattern that is perhaps an immature recapitulation of the more advanced circular pathway achieved at the second level of deep Qigong practice. In this tenuous development, the pulse rises up chong mai, then descends along ren mai. When this happens, the student is best advised to focus on the descending phase, since the chief aims at this point are to open ren mai, to build dan tian, and to rid the body of sick qi.

Sick Qi and Bad Karma

In his autobiography Paramahansa Yogananda describes how his guru once became ill as a result of taking on an excessive amount of bad karma from his disciples. Some yogis physically die as a result of taking on the burden of too much extraneous bad karma. Qigong masters suffer similar fates and must be able to withstand the sick qi they absorb from their students. Sick qi is Qigong's version of bad karma.

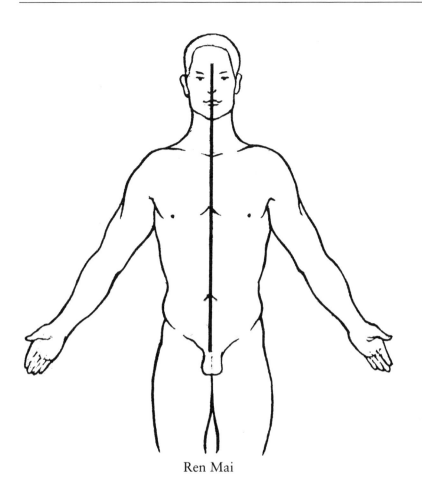

Ren Mai

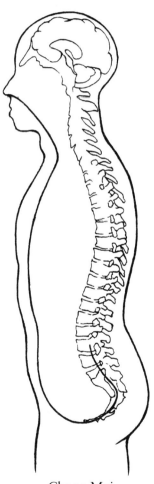

Chong Mai

Figure 24. *The pathway of ren mai, which runs along the body's surface, and chong mai, an internal channel running along the same general pathway.*

For this reason, both yogis and Qigong masters have tended to be very selective with their students, from whom the utmost respect and loyalty is expected. In both traditions, the masters test students for years before teaching them substantive techniques. Prospective yoga disciples must prostrate themselves before the master. Chinese Qigong and wushu require the student to *koutou,* or kneel and bow the head to the floor in front of the teacher. The Chinese word for disciple is *tudi,* which means "unarmed little brother." Student submission shows gratitude for the master's willingness not only to give up secrets but also to take on the student's physical and spiritual diseases.

Submission also demonstrates a willingness on the part of the student not to create conflict for the teacher, who can become a magnet for what psychotherapists call transference to describe what happens when a patient transfers latent resentment and hostility to the therapist. The patient's tendency to transfer often increases as the therapist begins to make headway in illuminating the patient's psychological disorder. In Qigong a psychologically troubled student is likely to experience transference when the teacher is close to liberating dan tian, which, because of its primacy at birth, is linked with both sexual feelings and childhood emotions. When a Qigong teacher activates the dan tian of a mentally balanced student, the student's feelings may range from overwhelming joy or sadness to mild pleasure. These feelings smooth out quickly, however, as the student's emotions give way to the sense of ren mai rising and falling.

Mentally unbalanced students are another story. They might become insecure and fearful, or they might go in the opposite direction, their physical self-confidence and sexuality becoming unwieldy. Attractions to others may feel overwhelming, or an indomitable self-love may take over the student's personality. In either case, problems between student and teacher are likely to emerge at this point, if they haven't already.

It is quite common and natural for students of the opposite sex to feel strong attraction for the teacher. When this happens, the teacher must be fully aware of the student's feelings and take quick action to help the student understand such feelings. If the student is insecure and fearful, then the teacher must assure the student that feelings of attraction are normal and nothing to be ashamed or frightened of. If the student is overly confident, the teacher must work to diffuse any infatuation. The teacher should regard such students as vulnerable younger brothers and sisters. Teachers who fail to take these steps can become, sometimes without their knowing, cult leaders. Drunk on their power over others, they feed off of the minds and emotions of their students out of vain, delusional self-aggrandizement.

When an unbalanced student becomes similarly narcissistic, the transformation may resemble an Oedipal crisis. Usually such students are of the same sex as the teacher, but not always. The first warning sign is resentful or hostile behavior toward the teacher. This indicates that the student is jealous of the teacher's controlling position, and if left unchecked, the jealousy may drive the student to symbolically "slay the father." This period of rebellion can take the form of critically scrutinizing the teacher's behavior for inconsistencies and missteps, arguing with the teacher over basic rules of practice, or simply ignoring the teacher's instructions so that the teacher is forced to confront the student in pointless, enervating debate. The trouble can, of course, get worse, which usually results in either the teacher asking the student to leave or the student quitting. This phase is especially unpleasant for the teacher, who may resent having to both instruct and absorb sick qi from someone who is apparently ungrateful.

Fortunately for people who want to study Qigong, teachers such as Zhang have taken on the added burden of instructing the "unworthy," who may then in turn try to educate other, more resistant types on the benefits of both trust and deep-level meditation practice. Though I may have been less resistant than most, I had days when I challenged Zhang's teachings. Once Zhang got so angry after I disagreed with him that he refused to meet with me for over a week. It wasn't until I got a taste of my own medicine as a teacher that I understood why Zhang and other Qigong masters require such unconditional respect and loyalty. Trying to instruct someone who has the semiconscious agenda of being troublesome is both a frustration and a waste of precious time that could be spent instructing more receptive students.

For a Western Qigong teacher, such an option is unrealistic. In the West skepticism and contentiousness are almost universally valued. It seems part of our birthright and heritage to rebel. Under such cultural conditions, Qigong teachers in the West may as well expect resistance to be the norm rather than the exception, which is the exact opposite case in China.

If Western students prove to be open and receptive, how pleasant the surprise for the teacher.

The Small Universe

The second stage of deep Qigong practice involves moving qi in the body in a pattern known as *xiao zhou tian,* or "small universe" (figure 25). In some Qigong systems, such as the one I studied prior to going to China, xiao zhou tian, usually translated as "microcosmic orbit," is the first thing the Qigong student attempts. As a result, students rarely gain control over their health to the extent that would be possible if they were able to sustain a lower abdominal pulse in dan tian and bring it up ren mai to the middle of their foreheads. Zhang's method takes care to ensure a degree of power in the student's dan tian, because without a developed dan tian the student can't circulate qi effectively along the small universe. Instead the student will simply dissipate his or her qi in trying to achieve the small universe.

After working with ren mai for six months, however, the teacher can help the student open a channel running up the back of the spine called *du mai,* sometimes translated as "governing pulse" or "channel." Du mai contains a number of significant points along its path. Of these, *ming men* (gate of life), located around the fifth lumbar, and *bai hui* (hundred meeting places), on top of the head, are generally acknowledged in other Qigong systems. The other points are sometimes emphasized, sometimes not. These points are associated with an array of human faculties and virtues.

The lowest point on the small universe is called *hui yin,* or "meeting place of yin qi," situated on the perineum. The next point, located at the coccyx, is *wei lü,* or "ox's tail." After that comes *ming men.* All three of these lower points correlate to physical power and sexuality. When they activate, the student may feel again a surge in physical strength and lust. Though the experience of the previous six months in the first level makes conflicts with the teacher less likely, students are still at risk as far as other people are concerned. Swaggering with their newfound power, they may try to demonstrate qi to their friends or entice members of the opposite sex into unwholesome relationships. For this reason, second-level students

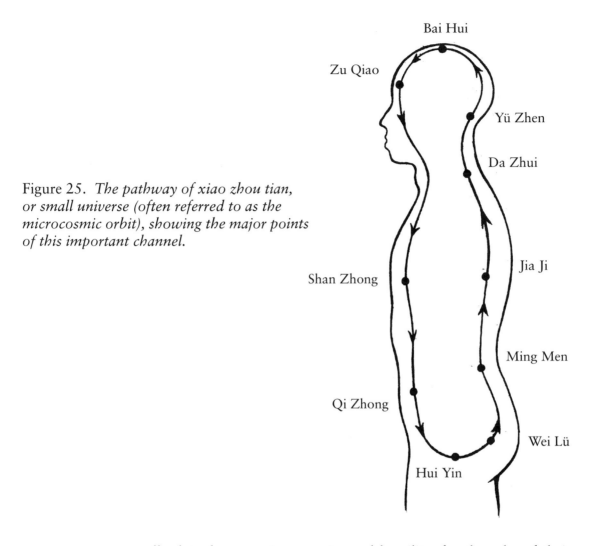

Figure 25. *The pathway of xiao zhou tian, or small universe (often referred to as the microcosmic orbit), showing the major points of this important channel.*

are well advised to practice restraint and humility, for the sake of their own development if not for the sake of others.

At ming men, the lower sexual qi changes in quality from physical to more spiritual and moves up to the higher regions. *Jia ji,* or "center of the spine," corresponds to human compassion and capacity to appreciate beauty. This area is also important in developing the ability to send qi to the arms and legs. Next occurs *da zhui,* or "big cone" (as in "pine cone"), a metaphor for the seventh vertebra. There compassion and aesthetic abil-

91

ity become articulate creativity, the power to express emotion and ideas.

For the head, there are three significant points. First comes *yü zhen,* or "jade pillow," near the medulla oblongata, then *bai hui* at the top of the head, followed by a point in the center of the forehead known as *zu qiao,* which means "ancestral key" but is also called the upper dan tian. Once these three head points are activated, qi has reached its highest development. Many Qigong masters, including Dr. Yan Xin, associate the opening of these head points with psychic or clairvoyant powers, such as seeing the future, reading another's thoughts, visualizing the inside of one's own or another's body, and automatically healing the sick. Yan warns against using these psychic abilities, because they can be depleted. For this reason, he says, the ancients kept quiet about their powers, storing up energy in order to live longer and accrue wisdom. The rationale for humility, then, is self-preservation.

My own experience has led me to cautiously accept such possibilities, though I feel it is highly unlikely that a person practicing Qigong for less than two years can sustain psychic powers. If a student quickly claims to have such power, it seems more likely that the self-aggrandizing impulse is at work. Fed by the large amount of printed material on Qigong, yoga, and other esoteric practices, students' fantasies about themselves often exceed their real abilities. Whenever I told Zhang about experiencing something beyond my means, he would smile and politely ignore me. If I pushed for a response, he would tell me that my Gongfu wasn't powerful enough to get excited about anything. I should just keep practicing and get stronger. Because of my many years in the martial arts and exposure to Chinese medicine and Taoism through publications in the West, I was irked by this treatment. From what I had been taught, people adept at Qigong could not only circulate qi throughout their entire bodies but could strike with superhuman devastation. My former Karate teacher was studying Qigong for the express purpose of being able to "punch through a brick wall." From time to time, I felt the need to remind Zhang of such things. His response was to look away or change the subject.

By the end of my first year in China, I had given up on broaching the subject of the martial arts applications of Qigong with Zhang. Then one evening he invited me to a "hard-style" Qigong demonstration being held at Beijing University. An entire family of hard-stylists, dressed in glittering circus costumes, performed a variety of stunts to prove the efficacy of their Qigong. A young fat man held rocks in his palm and then smashed them with his fist. A thin, muscular woman knelt while her two brothers stacked bricks on her head, then broke them with a sledgehammer. A slight, soft-looking man who resembled Jerry Lewis impersonating a Chinese took off his shirt, climbed a ladder, then fell on a spear. After several rotations on the spear's point, the man leaped to the floor and revealed a bloody spot just below his xiphoid process. The patriarch of the family capped off the evening by breaking a three-foot-thick rock with his head. While I stared, oohing and ahhing with the rest of the crowd, Zhang spent most of his time reading a book.

After the show, Zhang explained his indifference. Such feats were common in China—the old way of demonstrating Gongfu—but hard-stylists paid a price for their showing off. Because they squandered their qi, they wouldn't live long. It was better to demonstrate Qigong through health and the performance of difficult wushu routines. If an old person could perform a routine that was strenuous for a youth, then the old one clearly had Qigong. If a person lived a long, disease-free life, then he or she too had Qigong. Zhang reminded me that I had already felt the result of practicing hard Qigong during my Karate training. In a young person, the loss of qi wasn't so noticeable, but by the early thirties, sometimes sooner, the damage begins to manifest. I had to admit that the hard-style Qigong family didn't look so hot. Their faces bore the marks of pain and dissipation. Though they were stupendously strong, none of them had Zhang's healthy glow, and none of their demonstrations involved balance and grace. On top of that I had my own experience as proof. After a year, my wrist was back to normal, and I was healthier than I had ever been. Since that time I have neither seen nor experienced anything to make me feel that Zhang was wrong about hard-style Qigong.

Qigong masters typically try to dissuade their students from seeking superhuman power, physical or psychic. To discourage my students (and myself) from such thoughts, I follow Zhang's admonishment to focus on health. To that end, I offer a more practical advice with respect to the three head points of the small universe. The ability to make them pulse vividly means a high degree of mental and physical vigor and an absence of sick qi.

The middle dan tian—*shan zhong* ("middle of nipples")—is tied to its counterpart on the spine (*jia ji*) and so correlates to altruistic and aesthetic capacity, but shan zhong also has to do with selfhood, the core personality, which Taoism refers to as "spirit," believed to reside in the heart and pericardium. Chinese medicine uses the term "troubled spirit" to apply to a wide variety of mental and personality disorders. Because the middle dan tian includes the heart and pericardium, its growth and proper functioning, then, are vital for good mental health, which is inseparable from physical health. I find that many Westerners are particularly weak in the middle dan tian region. The West's high rates of heart disease, divorce, and emotional troubles might be manifestations of debilitated shan zhong areas.

The lower dan tian also goes by the name of *qi zhong,* or "middle of navel" (*qi* in this case means "navel," not "life force"). But qi zhong is also the preeminent place of order, the source of the lower dan tian, where the entire small universe originates and returns. If it is disrupted somehow, then the small universe ceases to flow. In combating illness in both myself and in others, I have noticed that the greater the illness, the weaker the lower dan tian seems to be. This weakness can manifest itself as physical flaccidity, as an energetic dullness, or as a negligible pulse. Small wonder, therefore, that many lethal blows in martial arts are aimed not at the genitals or at some other vulnerable part of the anatomy but at the lower dan tian itself.

The specific points along the map of the small universe are both guidepost and focus for students. When du mai opens, the student may not feel the specific points along the spine, just a general sense of the pulse in dan tian moving around the small universe. It takes time, practice, and specific methods to feel each point. After obtaining that feeling, it takes even more practice to become fully accomplished.

At this point, it is important to reiterate that safe, effective deep-level Qigong practice should be learned from a qualified teacher who can demonstrate the ability to move the lower abdominal pulse along xiao zhou tian. No one should attempt these practices solely on the basis of books or video tapes, which are by definition secondary sources. And while teachers who merely show people Taiji-like movements perform a good service, without the pulse in the lower dan tian they can do nothing more than offer the most rudimentary introduction to Qigong. And those who attempt to impart qi without paying sufficient dues—that is, at least two solid years of methodical, supervised Qigong training—can harm both themselves and others.

The Big Universe

The third level of deep Qigong practice entails circulating qi throughout the entire body along the path of *da zhou tian,* or "big universe." The big universe begins in the lower dan tian, from which qi descends on the exhale down the inside of the legs to the middle of the feet. On the inhale, the qi rises from the heels of the feet, up the back of the legs and the back itself. At this point the inhale is complete. From here an exhale causes the qi to branch and flow out the backs of the arms to the outside of the hands. Then, on the inhale, qi moves up the insides of the arms to the throat and goes around to the back of the neck and up to the top of the head, from which it finally culminates in the middle of the forehead. From there, the exhale sends the qi down ren mai to the lower dan tian and down to the feet, where the cycle repeats itself. (See figure 26.)

In the initial stages of the big universe meditation, as in the first two levels, students often find it more difficult to make qi descend than to make it ascend. In the West, this difficulty might be expected in people that habitually subordinate yin (descent) to yang (ascent), but I believe the difficulty is not limited to the West. Yin simply seems the more difficult of the two dialectical forces to master.

Like the initial experience of the small universe, the first sensations of the big universe are vague and general, but over time, with persistent, lengthy meditations (sometimes lasting two hours), the sensation grows more vivid. Eventually, the student can touch any part of the body and feel a slight pulse as qi moves through the spot being touched.

Zhang waited a year before he introduced da zhou tian to me. The first sign that I was ready for this level was a spontaneous warm sensation that flowed down my leg, as though I had spilled a warm drink on myself. After a while, I found that I could control this sensation with either my breath or my mind. Eventually, I could gain the sensation from practicing

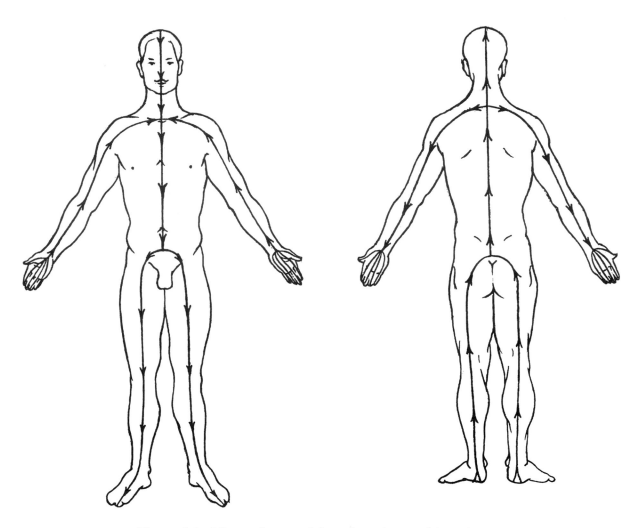

Figure 26. *The pathway of dao zhou tian, or big universe.*

Taiji or the Qigong movements, but only by long, difficult meditations was I able to move the sensation vividly around the big universe. In this third level, distractions have a more disruptive effect on the flow of qi. To traverse the big universe, one has to have a calm mind. Once a practitioner begins to feel da zhou tian, he or she can get a better sense of the entire qi field both filling and surrounding the body.

12

POWER, RESTRAINT, AND SPIRITUALITY

In his autobiography, Paramahansa Yogananda points to several instances where Christian saints and Hindu yogis show the same remarkable abilities, such as going for long periods without food or water, levitating, teleporting objects, and dematerializing. High-level Qigong masters make similar claims. Losing the appetite yet still remaining vital is a commonly touted side effect of deep Qigong practice. In Qigong, levitation goes by the name *qing gong,* or "light Qigong": the ability to decrease the body's weight so that insubstantial surfaces can be walked on. While living in Beijing, I witnessed a qing gong demonstration that was nationally broadcast over Chinese television. The Qigong master stretched a sheet of ordinary cellophane wrap between two supports and walked from one side to the other. As for teleporting objects and dematerializing, Dr. Yan Xin insists that such potential exists. I have never seen a demonstration of these abilities, but I don't dismiss them out of hand.

For me, out of all the claims of extraordinary power that come with practicing Qigong, the most striking notion is that Qigong might make the practitioner more spiritual—that is, more of a *spirit*—or more energetic. In this sense Qigong may be a kind of transubstantiation, a method of converting the matter of the body into spiritual energy. If deep-level Qigong does indeed transubstantiate flesh into spirit, then it seems logical that the practice, like kriya yoga, has remained in the hands of a relative few, whose austere and ascetic lives provide a natural barrier against the rest of humanity, greedily scurrying to satisfy its appetites. In fact, success at Qigong may depend on the practice of asceticism, at least to a degree. A practitioner's failure to think, feel, and act in accordance with the increase in spirit might conceivably lead to its loss. Like the ambitious Icarus, ignoring his father's warning not to fly too high, an arrogant Qigong adept might take wing, only to crash unexpectedly.

This was apparently the case with the two men who were "punished by heaven" for abusing Three Emperors Qigong. According to Zhang, each man, separated by a generation, grew arrogant and abusive when their Qigong powers reached a certain level of development. They not only took to brawling but used their martial arts to become proficient bandits. Both ignored the school's warnings against ambition, arrogance, and tyranny. Each man died suddenly without explanation.

To help keep Qigong upstarts in check, Taoism imposes restraints that closely resemble those sanctioned by Christianity, Judaism, and Hinduism. All three traditions urge humility, deference, compassion, kindness, and chastity or marriage to counteract vices such as pride, jealousy, wrath, greed, and lust. All three have evolved enormous volumes of literature on the subjects, the reading of which provides greater insight, hence mastery, over human weaknesses and strengths. But most important, each of the three prescribes internal practice as the ongoing solution to taming base impulses. Jews and Christians call their practice prayer; Hindus call theirs yoga; Taoists call theirs Qigong. Each traditional practice has various levels of efficacy and profundity, including miraculous powers.

Qigong, like other internal practices such as Hindu yoga and Buddhist meditation, spells out the source of its purported powers. According to the Taoist model, qi is stored and developed around the three dan tians (especially the lower dan tian), which are connected by the conception and governing channels (ren mai and du mai). This model correlates to the Hindu chakra line and the Buddhist notion of the *vajra* body, which closely resembles the Taoist system of channels and points, the smooth, unobstructed operation of which promotes mental and physical health. Moreover, in all three traditions, only diligent training will yield for the practitioner the full physical, mental, and spiritual benefits.

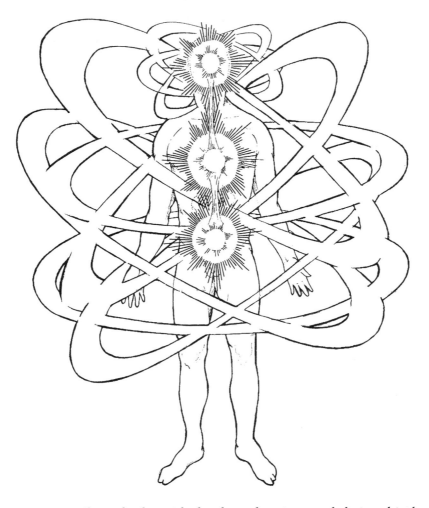

Figure 27. *The qi body, with the three dan tians and their orbitals.*

The one thing that separates Qigong from its sister internal practices is the way that it incorporates formal movements, particularly of the hands, which are actually the basis of Taijiquan. Each time the hands make a smooth, paintbrushlike pass through the air surrounding the body, the practitioner can feel the subtly fluctuating orbits of qi surrounding the waist, shoulders, and head, the three general locations of the dan tians. Even if the practitioner's sensitivity isn't acute enough to feel the dan tians and their orbitals, knowledge of their theoretical existence can lend a sense of precision to the trajectory of the hands and help clarify an overall pattern in the movements. In fact, the movements can expand the scope and enhance the fluidity of these external belts of qi. As the three dan tians and their orbitals grow through both movement and meditation, awareness of the entire "qi body" grows, giving the practitioner the concrete sensation of being immersed in pleasantly warm fluid. (See figure 27.)

The ability to feel and work with the orbitals that surround the three dan tians marks an important step in experiencing Qigong as a spiritual practice. Once the student begins to feel external sheaths of energy coursing across the palms and fingers, a sense of both wonderment and appreciation of his or her own existence may ensue, which in turn increases as the sense of qi becomes more of a certainty. At such a stage of confidence, the student is then better prepared to both sacrifice the time and adopt the behaviors that help make Qigong a profoundly spiritual practice.

13

FIGHTING
SICK QI

Dᴜʀɪɴɢ ᴍʏ ᴛɪᴍᴇ ɪɴ ᴄʜɪɴᴀ, ɪ ɢᴇɴᴇʀᴀʟʟʏ ꜰᴏᴜɢʜᴛ against sick qi on two fronts. The first was my wrist injury. The second front is known in the West as an upper respiratory infection. During the time I was practicing the automatic movements, I experienced both forms of sick qi as cramps in various parts of my body. With my wrist injury, sick qi manifested itself as a sharp pain in my liver and right kidney. Similarly, a head cold might show up as a deep ache either beneath the scapulae or at the back of the neck.

The practice of sitting meditation revealed similar responses as well. With both ailments, I felt itches and prickles shooting out of the pores of my skin. With respiratory infections, however, the sensations occurred more often in the head, like thousands of microscopic insects scuttling from eyes, ears, nose, and mouth. Occasionally my scalp erupted with hives, blisters, or tiny boils. Sometimes I was able to exert my qi to the extent that I drove what seemed to be an invading energy to the surface of my skin and into the surrounding air, at which point I felt as though the energy were still attached by tenuous tethers to my face. Scientific proof notwithstanding, sick qi, like healthy qi, feels electromagnetic, but unlike healthy qi, sick qi feels alien to the body.

A good way to visualize the difference between healthy and sick qi is to think of undamaged and scarred mucous membrane tissue. Healthy mucous membrane is pink, moist, supple, and smoothly surfaced: qualities that healthy qi recapitulates on the energetic level. Scarred mucous membrane, the incarnation of sick qi, is duller, drier, harder, and more irregularly surfaced. Moreoever, scarred mucous membrane's pitted surface allows foreign bodies such as viruses, bacteria, and pollen to more readily adhere than does the smooth, slippery surface of healthy mucous membrane. The frayed, irregular structure of sick qi, then, may very well be the means by which external disease is able to attack the body. Furthermore, if disease, like the body itself, is an energetic phenomenon, then its energetic shape may also have a similar irregularity, permitting it to bond with a like structure. A logical solution would be to smooth out the irregular structure so that it resembles the regular structure of healthy qi. This is the primary effect of practicing Qigong.

In both practicing and teaching Qigong, I have gained considerable respect for the dangers and complexity of sick qi. It can affect both student and teacher in a myriad of ways, but superficially almost all sick qi feels the same: an invisible lump, leaving a prickly after-sense. In detecting sick qi, the palms of the hand become another way of knowing—they become Geiger counters. The prickly, lumpy feel of sick qi is universal, whether the nature of the physical illness is cancer or the common cold. When people first begin to practice Qigong, the "tingling" that many report experiencing is actually the sensation of sick qi. This suggests that most everyone is full of sick qi. For that reason, the origin of sick qi bears investigating.

The Origins of Sick Qi

In some respects the Taoist concepts of human woes and natural law resemble those of the Romantic poets of England and America in the late eighteenth and early nineteenth centuries. Both the Romantics and the Taoists believed that children are born in a pure state, imbued with natural wisdom, which time and the vicissitudes of growth eventually dissipate. To stave off this dissipation or even to recover lost wisdom, the British and American Romantics prescribed solitude, immersion in nature, and rejection of the intellect and restraint in favor of imagination and passion. The Taoists prescribed Qigong, which may or may not include the prescriptions of the Romantics.

But even faithful practice of Qigong may not produce the needed results. The practitioner may have an inherited imperfection or condition that requires years to remedy. When I got proficient enough in both Qigong and Chinese to suit Zhang, he shared with me his view on the origin of such inherited problems, which were, he said, the result of "bad jing." Parents who lead bad lives, who were perhaps the children of bad parents, who were also the children of bad parents, and so on, bequeath bad jing to their children. This inheritance of bad jing means a child might be deficient in body or in mind, depending on the crimes committed by the parents. This principle recapitulates Western theology as well as scientific fact. Christianity asserts that the "sins of the fathers" will redound to subsequent generations, and in the past century science has found that many diseases have genetic causes. Even disorders that appear more psychological than physical, such as alcoholism and sexually violent or abusive behavior, seem to be transmitted from generation to generation.

Thus Zhang's concept of bad jing isn't too far afield from what the West already believes, and in keeping with the West's cautiousness with regard to absolute cause-effect relationships, Zhang counseled extreme discretion on this issue. He defined crime as simply a violation against the laws of the Three Emperors—heaven, human being, and earth—yet these laws are so complex, multileveled, and mutable that Taoist, Buddhist, and Confucian scholars devoted their entire lives to deciphering and codifying them. Crime, like sick qi, might take a lifetime to understand. In addition to this complexity, "bad" parents could unconsciously conceal their "crimes" through guile or false humility, in which case their child's misfortune might appear reckonless. In this way the remote cause-effect laws of heaven, human being, and earth fade into obscurity and disbelief.

If a child manages to be born with relatively untainted jing, then six deleterious emotions lie waiting to unbalance the body's zangfu. The first of these unbalancing emotions is fear. If allowed to persist by insensitive or uncaring parents, fear drains the kidneys and causes imbalance. Next, excess exhilaration—typified by the hyperactive behavior children exhibit around age two—weakens the heart. Anger upsets the liver. Morbidity weakens the lungs; worry, the spleen-pancreas. If a child is lucky enough to escape the devastations of all these pitfalls, the travails of adolescence await, the brunt of which is absorbed by the pericardium, designed to protect the heart from the shocks of failed love. Once a person becomes sexually active, orgasm joins the deleterious collection of harmful "emotions."

Sexuality bears a discussion all its own because of its profound place among human drives. Western science places sex alongside hunger as perhaps the deepest and most uncontrollable urge. Christianity, Islam, Hinduism, Buddhism, Taoism, Confucianism, and other religious traditions alternately glorify and condemn sex. As the source of procreation, sexual intercourse becomes in the eyes of religious traditions a divine mechanism for begetting souls and fostering familial love. As a supreme distraction and temptation, sexuality poses a threat to the same traditions. As far as Taoism and Qigong are concerned, the problem of sexuality is at base a physical one, especially for males, who during orgasm ejaculate fluid that for Taoism is the body's most precious substances: jing. Females also lose jing through orgasm, but the loss is far less severe. Their greatest drain occurs through menstruation and childbearing. Because men can experience orgasm many more times than women menstruate or bear children, ancient Taoists prescribed a schedule for male ejaculation that becomes increasingly prohibitive with age. From the ages of sexual springtime to the middle twenties, the effects of ejaculation are negligible. Once into the thirties, however, frequent loss of jing begins to take its toll. According to Taoist Qigong theory, the steady drain of jing results in balding, graying, wrinkles, lower back pain, leg pain and weakness (especially of the knee and ankles), and general loss of vitality.

The Taoists also believe that heterosexual intercourse performed according to certain principles can reduce the draining effect of orgasm on both male and female. Taoists interpreted the sexual relationship between men and women in terms of the yin/yang dialectic. If men protrude and express at the groin, then women open and receive at the groin. Conversely, if women protrude and express at the breast, then men open and receive at the breast. Since sperm is such a richly vital fluid, receiving a man's ejaculation can actually strengthen a woman. Likewise, since the female breasts are the counterpart to the penis, a man can receive a wom-

104

an's orgasmic qi through the middle dan tian. In this way men can gain a boost from women through sex.

The female breast makes a logical counterpart to the male penis in another way. Like the penis during orgasm, the breast, during and after pregnancy, exudes fluid—breast milk, which sustains the lives of infants. Recent studies indicate that women's health might benefit from breast-feeding. While this may be true, too much breast-feeding would, according to Taoist theory, have a draining effect similar to that of ejaculation on men.

All this supposes that the jing being exchanged between partners is healthy, which isn't often the case. When an unhealthy man injects his jing into a woman's womb, he contaminates her with a dose of his psychosomatic unhealthiness. Likewise, the unhealthy woman damages the man with her unhealthiness during intercourse. Moreover, sick qi and sexuality are linked by the fact the genitals are designed not just for sex but for urinating, a physical manifestation of sick qi. One of the terminals of the "conception channel," whose primary job is to eliminate sick qi, is at the genitals. Consequently, sick qi often shows itself in the body through aberrations in the genital region, particularly around hui yin, which is especially suited for the elimination of sick qi. As a Qigong practitioner becomes increasingly adept at driving sick qi from the deeper layers of the body, tiny, benign skin growths, or keratosis, may appear on or around the genitals. Keratosis can also occur under the arms or around any other significant lymphatic areas. With persistent practice, however, the keratosis disappears, a sign that the Qigong practitioner is approaching a degree of purity. If the tiny growths remain, the nature of the sick qi might be quite serious, indicating a more profound level of illness. It might take years of steady practice to prevail over the sick qi.

The tight relationship between sick qi and the genital region constitutes a great health threat for "alternative healers" who work with "energy." These healers are essentially attempting to manipulate qi, which on the deepest level consists of jing. Wilhelm Reich called it orgone. Freud called it the libido. What you choose to call it isn't as important as understanding its cause-effect nature. In order to successfully enhance a patient's energetic condition, a healer must have a high degree of control over his or her own libido or jing. Moreover, such a healer must be able to tolerate the patient's sick qi, which enters the healer's body through the various channels, especially those that run into the fingers. Unless the healer's own qi is quite strong, the sick qi will penetrate deeply into the internal organs and settle into the genital region. Many of the alternative healers I have met and worked with suffer from chronic lower back pain (kidneys), urinary tract infections, breast lumps, and menstrual irregularities. In severe cases women healers can develop genital tumors or might be forced to have hysterectomies. The danger for men lies in possible cancers of the penis, testicles, or prostate gland. Minor but worrisome side effects for both sexes include arthritic sensations and skin rashes, especially affecting the hands.

For this reason the Taoist Qigong tradition, along with the traditions of the Hindus and Buddhists, set rigorous standards for who should and who shouldn't heal others by energetic means. Many members of the rapidly growing—and in some cases specious—alternative healing community rarely measure up to these ancient and venerable standards. In my opinion, alternative healers who can't manifest the pulse in the lower dan tian and move that pulse along the microcosmic orbit can't effectively eliminate sick qi from their own bodies. Therefore, they might be harming themselves as well as their clients.* Such healers can pass sick qi to clients, who are unfamiliar with the nature of sick qi and so are unable to distinguish its effects. They may feel an initial surge of energy, the result of a "libido" transfusion. Oftentimes the healers themselves experience a surge as a result of the transfusion. In these cases the laws that determine who absorbs and who gets drained are uncertain. The only way to tell is to examine long-term results. If a person has gained deep-level Qigong ability, however, he or she can sort out more clearly the effects of such energetic transfusions. A Qigong adept who has absorbed sick qi may feel slightly dazed, even dizzy. Odd, tumultuous emotions are another sign.

---

*Over the past several years I have encountered quite a number of alternative healers and their clients with health problems that the Qigong model predicts. In spite of these problems, however, most refused to question deeply the relationship between their health problems and the alternative practices, perhaps a form of denial that stems from a combination of blind devotion and excessive ego involvement. Whatever the cause, the potential danger remains and should be seriously considered by both alternative healers and their clients.

If physical pain or discomfort is involved, then the sick qi can be quite destructive.

As strict as the Taoists, Hindus, and Buddhists are about who should use their energy to heal others, they are equally strict in dealing with the libido through sexual abstinence. By retaining libido or jing, the celibate grows stronger with each practice, regaining energetic ground lost long ago. The celibate who cultivates jing is more capable of synthesizing healthy qi from air and food, and thus is able to fight more effectively against virulent sick qi. By rechanneling the sexual urge through meditation rather than losing physical and eventually spiritual vitality through the quick thrill of orgasm, he or she can prevail over even the most stubborn of sick qi.

Given these constraints and difficulties, it is somewhat of a wonder that the Taoists concede that heterosexual intercourse, within certain limits, can promote health. Homosexuality, however, fails to fit into the yin/yang paradigm, so it can only lead to enervation. The same is true of masturbation, toward which the West takes a lenient stance. Many psychologists recommend masturbation as a method of relieving anxiety, a strategy that most of the Western world has probably already discovered for itself. If orgasm results in a loss of qi, chronic masturbators may be undermining their health. All of the Qigong masters I worked with in China demanded abstinence of their students. When I first began training with Zhang, he asked me to abstain from sex for a month. After I achieved the pulse in dan tian, he invited me to experiment. If I practiced within hours of ejaculating, the pulse moved with surprising force throughout my body. Aha! I said to myself, just another Chinese superstition. But as little as eight hours later, I was alarmed and dismayed to feel the pulse noticeably diminish. It took two or three days of abstinence and regular practice to recover.

In following out the Taoist logic on restrictions of male orgasm, men should withhold gratification for the sake of their own health and for the sake of their partners' pleasure. This way men retain their precious jing, while women get to indulge their greater capacity to experience orgasm. But men also run the risk of retaining dead jing, a stagnant accretion brought on by a number of near-climaxes. Dead jing usually results from abusing the method of jing retention. To help prevent the accumulation of dead jing, men should ejaculate after a number of near-climaxes. When a man becomes adept at retaining, he can follow sexual intercourse with a Qigong session, which can help distribute the jing throughout his body.

Even if all the harmful emotions, including the sex drive, could be managed, Chinese medicine identifies yet another source of imbalance in the zangfu to contend with: the six "external pernicious influences." These six environmental destabilizers are hot, cold, damp, dryness, wind, and summer heat, and each can invade and inhabit a weakened system. The yin/yang conditions of each organ determine the severity and nature of the invasion. A person with too much yang qi in the liver and a person with too much yin qi in the spleen-pancreas will not react the same to an invasion by "cold." The number of possible imbalances and the varied reactions caused by each external pernicious influence make diagnosis of illness a staggering job. No wonder Chinese physicians have to train for so long to practice effective medicine. But the goal of Chinese medical treatment is simple and singular: to restore "balance" to the patient's zangfu. Acupuncture and herbs provide more immediate relief, but the effects aren't lasting. To maintain a balanced system, the patient must practice Qigong faithfully and hope for the best.

So the terrible trilogy of bad jing, harmful emotions, and the six pernicious influences constitute the origin of sick qi. While working to expunge sick qi from the body, Qigong practitioners can maintain strength by taking certain commonsense steps. They can dress warmly in winter (especially in cold, damp weather) and avoid excessive heat in summer. They can eat regularly a diet rich in fresh, green leafy vegetables and grains, with adequate amounts of protein, drink only lukewarm or hot liquids (even in summer), and maintain emotional calm in the face of minor irritations.

Western science has championed many such commonsense remedies that were once a part of its folk tradition, especially remedies related to the mind. Like alternative healers, a whole new group of "mind-body scientists" has mushroomed, creating more opportunity for insight and confusion as well. Armed with a new encyclopedia of abstractions and machines, these mind-body scientists are busily reinventing what both Hindu yogis and Taoist Qigong masters long ago discovered. It doesn't seem too far-fetched to expect mind-body science to find that health and a calm, unagitated state of mind are synonymous. Nor does it seem unlikely that after billions of dollars and years of research, the emotions of fear, compulsive excitement, anger, worry, and morbidity will all be labeled destructive. But there may be an unforeseen complication as far as technology is concerned. Sick qi and electricity may be linked.

One spring morning in 1989, shortly before Hu Yaobang died and sparked the protests that would become the "Democracy Movement," I was practicing Changquan outside my living quarters, along the edge of a large pond called Nameless Lake. After I cooled down, I began doing Taiji in preparation for sitting meditation. Fish gurgled and splashed in the water. Languid willows draped their leafy branches onto the glassy surface. In the distance the giant pagoda that presides over Beijing University loomed splendidly in the unusually clean, morning air. Along the road the usual horde of elderly exercisers and Qigongers went about their peculiar business. Suddenly a commotion near the side of the building drew my attention as a crew of garrulous workmen struggled with what appeared to be an electrical problem. They had opened a fuse box and were debating loudly over whether or not it was too early to begin work, deciding finally to go around the side of the building and have a cigarette break.

As soon as they left, I walked over for a look, the qi so thick in my hands that I stopped and waved my hand at a shrub until I felt what seemed to be the plant's life force—magnetic, neither hot nor cold, something like a breeze. Out of curiosity I went up to the fuse box and emitted my qi, jumping when familiar cold prickles shot up my arm. Staring from hand to fuse box, I thought of the controversy over whether or not living close to power lines increases the risk of cancer. For a while I struggled with the supposition that electricity, the very lifeblood of the modern world, was in fact sick qi. I remembered as a child feeling deep terror whenever I saw giant segmented-insect-like power lines surging over the Alabama countryside. I began to believe that from the beginning evil had hidden itself in the very core of that which had so greatly improved the lot of the first few technological generations, building hope, only to close the pincers in a bitter surprise attack: electricity causes cancer.

When I shared this somewhat hysterical idea with Zhang, he responded that sick qi, though having a common *feel*, is too complex to be defined simply. It could be the result of too much or too little yang, too much or too little yin. It can be hot, cold, damp, dry. It can have too much or too little metal, earth, wood, water, or fire. He concluded that while there may be "some relation" between sick qi and electricity, strengthening individual qi was the central issue. That way the individual could resist the invasions of sick qi in all its multifarious forms.

Zhang's position seems reasonable. Even if Western science proved a link between electricity and cancer, for example, neither electricity nor technology are about to go away. Given the option of going without the convenience of technology, most people, I think, would balk. But in spite of technology's entrenched position in both today and the future, the ancient middle way of Qigong may emerge from the fray of mind-body research as the cheapest and most powerful solution to poor mental and physical health.

14

THE UNIFIED FIELD THEORY OF DISEASE AND LONGEVITY

In mid-April of my first year in China, I experienced most poignantly the harmful affect of the mind on qi. While making tea, I accidentally knocked over my cup and spilled hot liquid across my desk and a stack of papers I had been working on. I flew into a tirade, cursing and trembling as I reluctantly cleaned up the mess. Blood was pounding in my ears I was so angry, and I continued for several minutes to mutter obscenities over my bad luck. An hour or so later, when I went through my Qigong practice, I failed to get a pulse in dan tian. For three more days I went through practices with a lifeless dan tian. I had just learned the indispensable lesson that anger weakens the liver, which presides over the lower dan tian area and governs the movement of qi in the body.

From that time on, I began to ponder the significance of health as I was coming to know it through Qigong. I no longer associated the word with muscles, an absence of flab, or overt performance. *Health* took on a dimension that ramified out of the body and into the netherworld of the mind. A short time later I saw that health went even further: from the material world into that of the spirit.

A turning point occurred when Zhang, Liu Ziping, and I went to Dalian to a small teachers' college. Zhang had been invited to teach Qigong to about twenty physical education teachers, and I was tagging along to learn how to teach. We were met at the Dalian train depot by Mr. Fu, the head of the physical education department. Fu was a tall, muscular man dressed in tank top and baseball cap, and he was accompanied by a bulky, shiftless man named Chao, who wielded a certain degree of power in the area. Chao controlled—and thus effectively owned—a Chinese resort, a village of yurts, which he was making available to the Qigong classes. He also had a minivan and a private driver who took us to the yurt village, which sat on a grassy hill overlooking a beach on China's northeast coast.

By this time I had been in China long enough not to be intimidated by appalling sanitation, but the conditions of Chao's resort were worse than I expected. In the resort's restaurant, food was spat out or dropped carelessly on the dirty, damp cement floor, where it was left until the end of the day. Just outside the restaurant door, the cooks laid out goat carcasses on the road and sawed up the meat for the evening meals. One young cook got so drunk that he dropped an armful of empty beer bottles, then stepped onto the broken glass, cutting deep gashes in the soles of his bare feet. While I winced in horror, the cook sat down calmly on the dirt-crusted steps and simply wrapped adhesive tape around his feet. Later I saw him walking around, the tape soaked red with blood. Eyes tinkling with drunken cruelty, he picked up an air rifle and fired a pellet into the mangy hide of one of the few dogs I had seen while in China. The mongrel yelped, then fled behind a yurt while the young cook snickered and re-loaded.

I wasn't so much shocked at the filth or the cook's cruelty toward the dog as I was at the cook's lack of concern over exposing himself to infection. I fully expected him to die or to at least become horribly ill over a septic or staph infection, which no doubt thrived in the unclean environs of the yurt village. Every morning people from the summit all the way down the grade emptied their chamber pots, soaking the hill with urine, and no one seemed the least bit worried about it. Then there was the latrine, a hellish cement box divided by a foot-thick wall, open holes for toilets on one side, ice-cold showers on the other, a constant layer of slimy moisture coating the cold floor. The odor alone of the place was suffocating. Still, everyone seemed remarkably unaffected, even the cook, who remained drunk and apparently healthy throughout my two weeks.

The Qigong classes revealed another story. Many of the participants suffered from disease. One tough-looking short man, in an effort to explain his poor health, took my hand and squeezed my fingers over one of his nipples, which felt as though it contained a marble beneath the surface. Liu Ziping came over and translated what I had already felt: the man had lymphatic cancer. She then pointed out the rest of the students who had health problems. One potbellied older man had kidney cancer, several suffered from depression, and almost all of them had at one time contracted hepatitis. Inside the largest yurt, the classes began every day at dawn with a lecture from Zhang, and as Liu translated for me, I stared sadly at the twenty-odd participants. I even felt sorry for Chao and Fu, who seemed to be a far cry better off than the others. Both usually slept through at least half of Zhang's talk; everyone else seemed rapt. These talks brought together clearly much of the previous information I've already given on the lower dan tian and automatic movements.

Once Zhang had taught everyone the Qigong movements, my apprenticeship began. Everyone went through the formal movements, then immediately lapsed into crazed swaying and agitation. Liu and I followed Zhang around the yurt as he pointed out various students and the meaning of their movements. Most, he whispered, weren't really feeling Qigong, but he gave a significant nod to the potbellied older man who had kidney cancer. He shambled and careened like a resurrected corpse, and we watched him and the others for about ten minutes. Then Zhang crooned out orders for everyone to stand still, and he and Liu began working on the potbellied man. Liu stood behind the man, her palms hovering a few inches from the small of the man's back, at ming men. Zhang stood in front of the man and began stroking the air inches from the man's body, from the head, down the legs, to the ground. Then Zhang brought a hand over the man's heart and circled eighty-one times, then reversed the circles, also eighty-one times—the maximum amount of exposure to sick qi, I was later told. Next Zhang brought his hand across the man's chest to his liver, hand circling and recircling eighty-one times, after which Zhang ran his hand down the man's right leg, Liu simultaneously moving her hands down the backs of the man's legs. Later I learned that Zhang and Liu were applying the same yin/yang principle that enabled men and women to complement each other sexually. Their combined qi was stronger than the potbellied man's sick qi. The strategic placement of Liu Ziping behind also enhanced the yin/yang synergy. According to Zhang, ming men is an important sending and receiving area that responds especially to opposite-sex qi. If the person being treated were a woman, then Zhang would have stood behind while Liu manipulated qi along the front.

While they worked on the potbellied man, both Zhang and Liu made sour faces and afterward vigorously shook out their hands as though they were covered in some foul liquid. Then Zhang whispered in the man's ear, and the man thundered to the floor, flat on his back. Like a magician poised over his worthy assistant, Zhang waved his hands over the supine body. He knelt beside the man and repeated the circles over the heart and liver, his hand finally hovering over the man's dan tian, where he circled and recircled. Zhang pulled back his hand and used his first two fingers, aiming them like a gun at the man's dan tian. Wet, gurgling sounds came from the man's gullet, and I stared in wonderment as a faint pulse appeared just below the navel.

Zhang helped the potbellied man get up, then he lifted the man's arms in front of his chest and told him to keep them there. Zhang put one hand over the man's ming men, then traced a path up du mai to the top of the head, where one hand hovered over bai hui while the other stroked down ren mai, stopping at dan tian. There Zhang circled and recircled, pushing into the space in front of dan tian, then pulling back. A strange smile came to the potbellied man's face. Zhang withdrew his hands and walked quickly to a wall of the yurt, where he shook his arms repeatedly, vibrating and flinching, "casting away" the potbellied man's sick qi.

After a few minutes, Zhang told the students to open their eyes and had them go through the closing movement. Next Zhang gave instructions on sitting meditation. While the students sat with closed eyes, Zhang went around the room and aimed his right index and middle fingers at various students' dan tian areas. One of them—a short man with a bristly crew-cut—began to rock and mumble. A young woman erupted into shrill giggles. After firing qi at various students for ten minutes or so, Zhang went outside the yurt and shook vigorously. Then his movements slowed until

114

he swayed gently according to the patterns of the "belt" and "shoulder" orbits. Finally he returned to the head of the class and sat in a half-lotus position. When the meditation ended, Zhang led everyone through the same whole-body massage he had taught the night I glimpsed my first automatic movements. He said the massage was designed to spread qi that may have collected in various acupuncture points all over the body. In conclusion he explained how Qigong liberated long-buried emotions. Everyone nodded and meandered convivially out of the yurt and headed toward the restaurant for lunch.

We arrived to find that Chao had arranged something special, a veritable truckload of "red clams" he had managed to get from a local banquet being held for a group of Communist dignitaries. Fu slapped Chao on the back and said that Chao was the biggest man in Dalian. Everyone congratulated Chao, then we ate greedily. Both Chao and Fu tried to pull the scam of "get the foreigner drunk," but I remained moderate, which Zhang defended as part of being a "good disciple." I drank half a bottle of beer, and just when I was starting to enjoy a slight tipsiness, my belly began to feel unnaturally full.

I went back to my yurt for a lie-down, but when I woke, it was dark and my cot was drenched in sweat, my stomach swollen like a basketball. I rushed outside and vomited everything I had consumed at lunch. The entire yurt village was silent, lights visible in only a few of the felt tents. Zhang's was decidedly dark, so I returned to my hut, where I rinsed out my mouth with water from a thermos. Minutes later I was vomiting again. This time very little seemed to come up, and I lay on my soaked cot and shivered with chills. A sharp pain, as though I had swallowed glass, cut across my abdomen. It moved lower, until my bowels began to stir.

Armed with a flashlight, I stumbled hurriedly down the hill to the nightmarish latrine. In searching for a reasonably clean place to squat, my flashlight caught an army of slimy white maggots crawling up the hole. That night I had to return to the latrine so many times and in such pain that I regarded the maggots with near-indifference. All I knew was that my abdomen writhed in pain. Just before finally falling asleep, I panicked upon remembering that earlier that year a Shanghai hepatitis epidemic had been caused by clams, but I calmed myself with the vague assurance that hepatitis had an incubation period of several days. Even so, dysentery by itself could be fatal, so I settled into the attitude that if I died, I had no one to blame but myself. Either Zhang and I would defeat the illness with Qigong, or I would perish.

The next day Zhang put qi into my gullet. He gathered the pain from the four corners of my abdomen and focused it into a knot that moved slowly with his hand down the snaky course of my intestinal tract. I got up and vomited again. Outside my yurt a group from the teachers' college, who had gathered when they saw Zhang go in, watched as I retched. They frowned sadly as I staggered back inside. Zhang helped me back to bed and said I had a "big problem."

"Stomach disease?" I asked, the Chinese expression for dysentery.

"Maybe," Zhang said. "Don't worry."

"Okay," I said.

But rest was next to impossible. Chinese tourists who had heard about the sick foreigner continually entered my yurt for a look. When Zhang finally succeeded in keeping them out, they formed a crowd beside my yurt and chatted for periods of time.

I spent the better parts of the next three days on my back. In the evening of the second day, I was able to drink boiled water. Up until then nothing stayed down. On the third day I ate a little cake. When I was finally strong enough to practice, I experienced unprecedented sick qi effusions.

During a particularly strong practice I had a vision of the plasmic swirl of my own qi like a spiral galaxy expanding outward from the central black hole of dan tian: the parameters of my "astral body." It was then that I realized that dan tian wasn't so much the soul itself as the place where the soul had materialized, sending out a plume of qi, which was actually the result of the spirit contacting the material. Though my qi and body had expanded with time to further extremities, one day it would contract until the qi gathered and spent over a lifetime collapsed into its point of origin. The purpose of life suddenly became clear to me: to create and accrue greater amounts of qi that would return to dan tian when the great contraction finally arrived.

Drifting from the dark border into the midst of this swirling life force were dull, angular lumps moving more slowly than the surrounding bright plasma. These were the sources of inertia and sickness that slowed the speed and spread of the swirl of life. Some lumps varied in size and were sprinkled throughout the qi field. They were diseases, which in cutting life short might conceivably rob the spirit of its chance to grow in preparation for the afterlife. The largest lumps were calamity (in which category the poisonous side of technology might be included), while the smallest but most numerous constituted the destructive emotions, pernicious environmental influences (another potential grouping for technologically induced disease), and "inherited sin," all of them prematurely slowing the centrifuge of the soul within the body so that the centripetal force of death could drag the last vestiges of the bright whorl into the hole from which the soul had been born.

In this way, in the midst of the expansion and contraction of the great whorl of the soul, every great and small disease, every calamity, destructive emotion, pernicious influence, and inherited sin was linked incrementally to death. The tiny granules at the outer fringes of the great whorl we call the common cold, Death's fingertips, indistinguishable from the pernicious emotion of "stress," the by-product of "fear," "ambition," "anger," or "greed." Larger fragments further inside the fringe represented illnesses such as influenza, its relative hepatitis, all the childhood diseases, and a plethora of viral infirmities, some of which have yet to be named. As the soul continued to unwittingly experience "little deaths" caused by these invading fragments, the motion of the whorl would become sluggish, contracting from the fringes toward the center where momentum was greater, mistakes more costly, and disease more virulent. Speed around and toward the center increased, as in the narrowing swirl of a vortex.

I saw then how Qigong could give the practitioner the power to fulfill life's purpose. It helped sustain motion in the fringes, awakened the human ability to fight against small diseases that might otherwise cause contraction, making susceptibility to deadly disease more likely. The Qigong practitioner could fight back against the physical and spiritual enemies of humankind.

While this stunning image lingered in my mind, it occurred to me with equal clarity that the moral nature of life force demanded more than simply creating and accruing qi to stay alive. The qi created and accrued would have to be of high quality, perhaps having palpable traits that could be felt through the practice itself. If a person remained alive a long while but did so by guile, greed, hypocrisy, and spite, then the qi that returned to dan tian would be "sick." An innocent child, whose qi was at its purest and most uncontaminated, would die to a better afterlife than would the stingy, greedy miser who lived a long, bitter life. If, however, that same greedy miser were to discover and practice Qigong—which necessitates decency, kindness, and peacefulness—then the qi returned to dan tian would be "healthier" than the qi developed from a lifetime otherwise led. Thus, the practice of Qigong might benefit not only the quality of this life but perhaps also that of the afterlife.

Years later and many experiences the wiser, I can say that my revelation was no hollow imagining. Using Qigong to engage such recurrent nuisances as colds and flu strengthens the sense of qi flowing around the small universe and builds resistance to infection. Though at one time I was plagued several times a year by the common cold, I can now use Qigong to effectively kill or contain the disease. My students enjoy a similar ability, but neither they nor I would have such ability if it weren't for the steady, devout practice of Qigong. The devotion to practice has other psychological benefits. It keeps harmful emotions at bay and puts the practitioner in a peaceful, happy state of mind, also conducive to health.

In teaching Qigong, I have had to project qi from my own body into the bodies of others, many of whom have had serious diseases. These include breast, prostate, and skin cancer; AIDS; multiple sclerosis; Crohn's disease; peptic ulcers; genital herpes; genital warts; chronic fatigue syndrome; osteoarthritis; rheumatoid arthritis; and a variety of undiagnosable problems, generally written off by both doctors and patients as "allergies," "skin rashes," and "part of the aches and pains of life." In every case, the same basic prickly sensation of sick qi emanated from the three dan tians and related acupuncture points, thus corroborating my vision that all diseases in the body share a common energy. That energy may simply be the signal that the body's immune system is trying to do its job. The continued presence of that energy accompanied by symptoms perhaps shows the body's immune system is failing. Western science implicitly confirms that all pathology is related by defining illness as the body's failure to repair itself.

15

PARTING
THOUGHTS

Zhang taught me that a good Qigong teacher commands dan tian, has strong legs, and shines with health, but before I came to China, I had only one good idea about what constituted a good teacher. I had made a pact with myself never to become the student of a teacher who didn't appreciate literature. It was an idea born of my experience with Karate and American martial arts. Unless the mind is guided by a sensibility higher than "might makes right," all efforts are doomed to failure.

After working with Zhang for a few weeks, I was fairly sure he was the kind of teacher for me, but I decided one night to visit and ask him a few pointed questions. Through Liu Ziping I asked if he had a favorite work of literature. After a quick exchange between them, I watched him nod as she answered that he had a favorite poem. Zhang got up and took out a double-edge sword and acted out the poem as Liu interpreted as best she could. He held the weapon vertically along ren mai and stood straight, a smile fixed to his ruddy face. "The poem describes the growth of a boy to a man," she said.

Zhang said a few words, then took two steps forward, still smiling, sword still in front of his body. "He grows from a child to a boy," Liu said. Zhang spoke again and took three steps forward. "He grows older, from a boy to a young man, twenty-five years old." Zhang uttered a few more sentences, then took four more steps until he was near the wall. "When he nears forty, the man looks back on the path he has made in his life."

Zhang turned around, raised a hand to his brow as though looking far off into the distance, then his face soured, shooing with one hand, holding with the other the sword, which he suddenly raised over his head, eyes watery and fierce. He took the sword with both hands and cleaved the imaginary path he had traced with his steps, the metal blade hissing and rattling from the force of the slice.

I never found out the name of the poem or the author because my Chinese was so poor that I wouldn't have been able to retain the information. But what I saw spoke much louder and clearer than words in any language. After my wrist finally healed, Zhang gave me a sword, and I practiced so much that I broke the solid metal bar that attached the handle to the blade. Consequently, Zhang let me borrow one of his, the same one with which he had demonstrated that night, and every time I picked it up, I remembered his less than subtle demonstration of what I had to do in order to learn deep-level Qigong. I had to stop loving the self that had blundered along the path of life without the aid of Qigong. Faced with the wall toward which my original trajectory had aimed me, I had no choice but to use the internal sword of ren mai to perform corrective surgery on myself. Unless I changed my ambitious, externally driven Western consciousness, I would fail.

On my last day in China, all the foreigners on Beijing University's campus were given two hours to pack two bags of luggage to carry away when their respective embassies came to collect them. The Tiananmen massacre was less than eight hours past. After I packed, I went over to Zhang's apartment to tell him what was happening. I had planned to remain in China for another three months to learn more. Zhang lowered his head and suggested that I stay in spite of the mass exodus. I explained I had no choice, after which he got up, and we rode bikes together back to my building, where a few foreign cars were loading up and leaving. Once in my room, Zhang picked up the sword he had loaned me. He pulled the sword from the scabbard and admired the blade.

"This sword is not real," he said. "It is nothing unless the hand that holds it has mastered Qigong."

Neither of us said anything for a minute while we stared at the sword. Then he wrote down several sentences in Chinese and said they were very important ideas that would help me perfect my Qigong. Unable to restrain my curiosity, I used my Chinese-English dictionary to translate the first sentence. It said, "If you want your body to be like a jewel, then never leave that happy place."

Fumbling for some way to reciprocate, I gave him several pictures of the two of us, then we shook hands. When he let go, I caught him by surprise with an embrace that left him rigid and confused. I knew that Zhang, like many traditional Chinese, would object to such a display of emotion, but I wasn't just embracing a man. I was showing my acceptance of a new way of life. Zhang had shown me that I had been wearing myself out by splashing along the surface of life. He had taught me to swim with grace and endurance.

As though he understood, Zhang's shocked expression faded, and together we strode from the room and went down the dark hall, which clacked and echoed with the sounds of foreigners packing. When we came out the front door, a gang of unfamiliar foreigners stood loading luggage into a small convoy of vans and cars with embassy tags. They wore white shirts and dark ties, and it was clear they didn't like their work. The embassy personnel stopped loading suitcases and stared while Zhang walked to his bicycle, sword in one hand, photographs in the other.

Zhang put the photos in his jacket pocket, held the sword across his handlebars, then waved goodbye. He pedaled away at the same easy pace he always traveled, and I watched until I could no longer avoid the stare of a tall, barrel-chested man with a trimmed beard. The man put his hands on his hips and asked in a Midwestern American accent what country I was from. I waited for a second, the sound of the man's voice strange to my ears, as though it were an unfamiliar language. The word *America* fell out of my mouth like a moan uttered just before sleep, and it seemed that I had never before said the word, and that when I said it again, it would never again seem strange.

Part Two

THE EIGHT MOVEMENTS OF THE THREE EMPERORS QIGONG

16

TESTING THE WATER

ONE OF THE MAIN TENETS OF THIS BOOK IS THAT QIGONG should be practiced with a good teacher. I stand firmly by this position. Readers should not delude themselves into thinking that deep-level Qigong can be achieved by imitating movements from a book.

That doesn't mean, however, that novices can't get their feet wet, so to speak, and to that end, the publisher has asked me to reveal the movements of the Three Emperors Qigong. These movements are the same ones that Zhang initially taught me, which, according to Zhang, "exercise the inner organs, conserve the qi of dan tian, and get rid of bad qi so that the good qi can move and help the organs relax and accumulate qi to overcome barriers." Of the eight movements, the third and fourth invoke the qi of fu organs. The other six arouse the qi of the six zang organs. Zhang explained that the eight movements were designed to draw upon the three sources of qi: air, food, and jing. In fact, the extremely light breathing forces the body to draw upon the deeper "breath" (jing or prana). As I progressed in my training, following the exact pattern Zhang originally prescribed became less important. To demonstrate the point, Zhang showed me other systems of Qigong movement, which at that level were just as effective in stimulating my qi. The original eight movements of the Three Emperors' system, however, get the best results of any other Qigong I have ever tried.

Though what I present here are the original Eight Movements of Three Emperors Qigong, I have taken the liberty of offering in parentheses alternate names for the eight formal moves. I came up with these names as a way of helping to explain the movements as I teach them. Because their function is purely practical, the names are unpoetically descriptive.

Tongue Position and Reverse Breathing

Curling the tongue to touch the upper palate and using reverse breathing are essential in practicing Three Emperors Qigong. Curling the tongue is a simple task. Just arch the tip of the tongue so that it naturally rests somewhere on the upper palate. Since tongue sizes differ, prescribing specific points of contact isn't very helpful. As for reverse breathing, consult figure 28, then try the following exercise.

While sitting or standing, place the hands over the lower abdomen just below the navel. Then, on the inhale, press the hands inward while you contract the lower abdominal muscles. On the exhale, relax both the hands and the muscles so that the lower abdomen protrudes into the hands. Don't force the lower abdomen out. Let it relax into expansion. Do this exercise for fifty complete breaths (one breath equals one inhale and one exhale) until reverse breathing becomes natural. During this time, keep the eyes closed and concentrate on your breath, which should be done slowly and lightly through the nose, the tip of the tongue resting comfortably against the upper palate.

A word of warning about reverse breathing. Some Qigong teachers recommend "yogic" or "Buddhist" breathing, the exact opposite of reverse breathing, which, they claim, can have "a harmful effect" on the student's qi. I have tried both methods, and, if done properly, reverse breathing is clearly superior. It engages more intensely the nexus of the descending aorta, the surrounding lymph glands, and the lumbar/sacral nervous system. In terms of the Chinese paradigm, reverse breathing more effectively draws upon the body's jing, stored in dan tian and the genital region.

Once you get the hang of reverse breathing, you are ready to begin the formal phase of Three Emperors Qigong: the eight primary movements. Each movement can be divided into two parts according to breath: the inhale phase and the exhale phase. Inhales occur either at the beginning

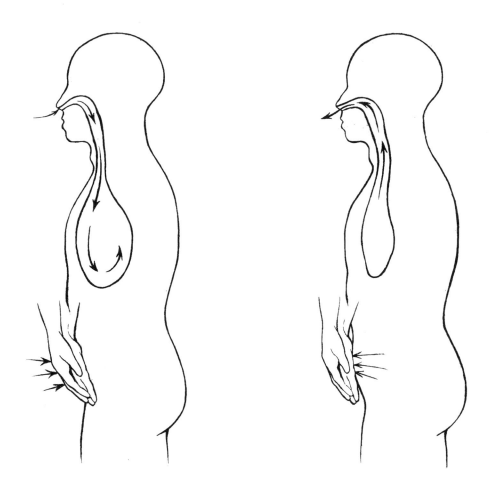

Figure 28. *Reverse breathing exercise:* (A) *inhalation and* (B) *exhalation.*

of a movement or during a transition from one movement to the next. Also, inhales are usually performed when the hands contract toward the body. Exhales usually occur when the hands extend. Whenever the body stoops, however, an exhale must occur, no matter what the hands do.

Before describing the Qigong movements, let me point out five things that all the movements share. First, each movement is performed three times. Second, all but the last of the movements are performed on both left and right sides, and in these cases motion commences to the left. Third, the movements to both left and right sides involve the hands, waist, and shifting of weight, all occurring at the same time, usually in the same direction. Fourth, all motion to left and right sides should originate from the waist or hips, so that arms and hands move as a consequence of waist or hip movement. And fifth, the hands, arms, and all of the upper body muscles should remain relaxed throughout. The relaxation of the upper body while the legs remain in a state of at least mild tension is characteristic of all forms of moving Qigong and internal martial arts. This condition reverses the sensibilities that typify a Western concept of "strength," which, I believe, center largely around images of the upper body. Western sports, such as football, basketball, and even track and field, understand and tout leg strength as fundamental, yet the upper body usually receives equal, if not preponderant, training, especially in the case of football. Other than soaking in hot tubs or receiving massage, the upper body is not encouraged to relax, particularly during the sport itself, when both upper and lower body remain in a state of constant tension and hyperactivity. Qigong's insistence on upper body relaxation and slow movement not only reverses the Western sports mind-set but in fact may bring about at least some of its health benefits. We know that digestion and metabolism happen more efficiently in a state of rest, and we know that the immune system often works best if stressful activity is reduced or eliminated, hence bed rest as the usual prescription for most common illnesses. Thus the peculiar arrangement of upper body relaxation and minimal stress on the lower half may induce in the nervous system an odd hybrid of rest and activity, both of which might affect digestion, metabolism, and immunity.

The Beginning

The opening movement of Three Emperors Qigong is the same as the opening movement of several Taiji forms. Before beginning, note the position of the feet, which should be about shoulder width apart, toes pointing straight ahead. This foot position is known as "forward-facing," a term essential in describing the movements of the legs and feet throughout the eight Qigong movements.

So, feet in forward-facing position, legs straight without being rigid, arms relaxed at sides, raise the arms upward to about collarbone level and inhale slowly. The arms should be straight without tension. The hands should be relaxed and bent at the wrist joints. All at once, drop the arms, slightly bend the knees, and begin a slow exhale. As the arms descend,

Figure 29. *Beginning:* (A) *forward-facing position,* (B) *raise arms,* (C) *drop arms and sink down, and* (D) *draw hands in toward the body.*

A

B

C

D

A   B   C

Figure 30. *First movement (to the left):*
(A) *begin circle,* (B) *farthest extension,* (C) *return.*

bend the elbows and flex the hands at the wrist joints, as though stroking a sheet of glass directly in front of you. The hands continue to drop until they are in front of the lower dan tian, at which point draw the hands toward the navel and inhale slowly. Aside from waking up the kidney qi, this movement represents both an effort to bring qi down to the lower dan tian and a descent from the upright world of yang into the downward, slow world of yin. The legs shouldn't be bent so as to create too much stress. This isn't the case in many athletic forms of Taiji, wherein the knees are bent to the extreme in order to build the quadriceps.

1. FORWARD-LEVEL CLOUD HANDS LEFT AND RIGHT (FORWARD CIRCLE LEFT AND RIGHT)

"Cloud Hands" (*yun shou*) is the name of a beautiful, lilting arm and hand action made famous in Taijiquan. The first four movements of Three Emperors Qigong bear this name because they share the characteristic

130

A   B   C

Figure 31. *First movement (to the right):*
(A) *begin circle,* (B) *farthest extension,* (C) *return.*

smoothness of the Taiji move, except that the Three Emperors Qigong movements operate on a "level" plane. Though the names of these moves are poetic, they don't translate well visually for Westerners. I have therefore given the movements names that more clearly describe what the hands do: in this case, forward circle left and right.

The hand motion of the first movement (figure 30) originates with a slow exhale from the lower dan tian, where the hands have been placed from the opening movement. As mentioned above, the movement commences to the left. On the exhale, the hands describe a low circular pattern that roughly coincides with the middle orbital of dai mai, the three rings of qi surrounding the lower dan tian. As the hands sweep to the left, shift the body's weight so that it sits primarily over the left leg; then, as the hands draw inward, inhale and shift the weight back onto the right leg. When the hands reach their original placement in front of the dan tian, turn the waist back to its original position. Repeat this action two more times; then in identical fashion perform three forward circles to the right (figure 31).

A   B   C

Figure 32. *Second movement (to the left):*
(A) *turn behind,* (B) *farthest extension,* (C) *return.*

The forward circle movements to the left help activate the qi stored in the spleen-pancreas, whereas the same movements to the right affect the liver's qi. In terms of the five-element ke cycle, the movements commence with earth, the controlled element, then proceed to wood, the controller. So the first set of movements blends these two elements, which according to the Chinese model have a "destructive" or "dominant-submissive" relationship.

Though the hands move along the plane of the middle orbital of dai mai, they pass through the intersection of the two diagonal orbitals when they return to the point of origin. Thus the hands engage all three orbitals of dai mai.

A   B   C

Figure 33. *Second movement (to the right):*
(A) *turn behind,* (B) *farthest extension,* (C) *return.*

2. REAR-LEVEL CLOUD HANDS LEFT AND RIGHT (REAR CIRCLE LEFT AND RIGHT)

After exhaling and completing the last forward circle to the right, inhale softly and turn the waist so that the body is in its original forward-facing position and the weight is equally distributed on both feet. Bring the hands back to the dan tian. Then, continuing to inhale, turn the waist left so that the whole body, including the hands, faces the rear, and at the same time shift the weight onto the right leg. Next, exhale and turn the waist back toward the front and shift the weight onto the left leg. At the same time trace with the hands the left-rear portion of the same qi orbital of dai mai engaged by the first movement. As the waist and hands return to their original, forward-facing position, take a long, slow inhale and move the weight from the left leg to equal distribution between left and right. (See figure 32.) Repeat this rear circular movement two more times; then perform three identical rear circles with commensurate breathing to the right (figure 33).

The rear circles continue the process begun with the forward circles: blending the qi of the spleen-pancreas (left) and liver (right), which is to say the earth and wood elements. The transition from the last right forward circle to the first left rear circle follows the natural order of controller (wood) to controlled (earth), but in going from left rear circles to right, the order of the ke cycle is again reversed as in the first set of movements.

As for the orbitals, the hands engage all three circuits just as in the first movement.

That the first two movements invoke and mix the qi of the spleen-pancreas (earth) and liver (wood) suggests that those two organ systems play an immediate role in the body's collective qi. In terms of emotion and everyday behavior, the psychosomatic qualities of both the spleen-pancreas and liver have a huge impact on human life: the spleen-pancreas serves like the earth as the seat of our capacity for contemplation and nurturance, and the liver acts like a sprouting tree as source of our need to expand and assert ourselves. When looked at in this light, the mental and emotional energies represented by the spleen-pancreas and liver inform virtually every waking moment of our lives, and like yin and yang they form a dialectic out of which our responses to the world emerge. The blending of the qi of these organ systems, then, helps the practitioner achieve a kind of neutral state of mind, where repose and ambition dissolve into one another.

The liver, or the wood element, is important for another reason. It not only circulates qi throughout the body but also governs the dan tian region. My experience has shown that inability to feel a pulse in the dan tian region is usually related to a problem in the liver (for example, stagnation). In such cases the universal cause seems to be an overabundance of rage, conscious or unconscious. How fitting, then, to cut this excess with the more passive energies of the spleen-pancreas. And in cases of the reverse condition—that is, an overly phlegmatic personality—the more aggressive essence of the liver can help dissipate psychological paralysis.

On a more visceral note, the spleen-pancreas and liver also play important roles in digestion, the major organs of which are invoked in the next two sets of movements.

3. INSIDE-LEVEL CLOUD HANDS (THE BREASTSTROKE)

The third movement (figures 34 and 35) closely resembles the breast-stroke. The last portion of the third rear circle right dovetails into the start of the breaststroke. After the waist and hands have returned to their original forward-facing position (inhale) so that the weight is distributed fifty-fifty between left and right, shift the weight to the right while simultaneously turning the waist left and pointing the left foot to the left. The hands are again in front of the lower dan tian, palms facing one another. Then, pushing gently off the right leg so that the weight moves onto the left, softly exhale and bring the hands forward, palms still facing each other, exactly as a swimmer "glides" while doing the breaststroke. When the arms are fully extended, begin inhaling, and separate the hands and bring them back to their starting position while turning the waist forty-five degrees to the right and shifting the weight from the left to the right leg. This movement parallels the "pull" segment of the swimming breaststroke and puts the body back into the same position from which the movement began. Repeat these actions and breathing patterns two more times; then, after completing the third movement to the left, inhale and shift the weight back onto the right and turn the left foot ninety degrees so that it becomes forward-facing. The hands sweep back to the lower dan tian. Then shift the weight onto the repositioned left foot and point the right foot to the right. Perform three breaststrokes to the right.

The third movement activates the qi circulating in the general fu organs, which include stomach, small intestine, large intestine, urinary bladder, gallbladder, and the triple heater. As members of the fu system, the qi of these organs is generally yang, which is associated with heat. The breast-stroke begins a process that continues into the fourth movement, which also promotes the qi of the digestive organs.

Unlike the first two movements, which seem largely focused on the middle orbital of dai mai, the third movement engages all three orbitals more fully—the middle one during the "glide," and the two diagonals during the "pull"—as well as the lower orbitals of the middle dan tian.

A

B

Figure 34. *Third movement (to the left):*
(A) *beginning,* (B) *farthest extension,* (C) *return.*

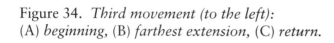

C

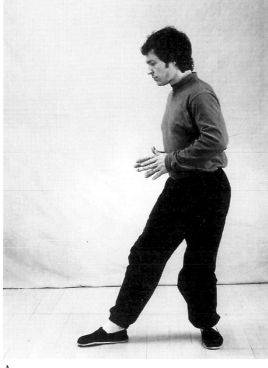

A

B

Figure 35. *Third movement (to the right):*
(A) *beginning,* (B) *farthest extension,* (C) *return.*

C

4. OUTSIDE-LEVEL CLOUD HANDS (THE BUTTERFLY)

The fourth movement (figures 36 and 37) also resembles a swim stroke: the butterfly. As far as the breath, legs, waist, and weight shifts are concerned, the movement is the same as that of the third. Only the relationship of the hands is different. In fact, the fourth movement reverses the hand relationship of the third movement, just as the butterfly swim stroke reverses the relationship of the hands of the breaststroke. The Chinese names capitulate this through the tags *inside* and *outside*.

The transition from the third to the fourth movement is the same as though the third movement were about to be repeated on the left. While slowly inhaling, transfer the weight onto the left leg, turning the right foot ninety degrees on the heel so that the foot is forward-facing. At the same time, draw the hands in toward the lower dan tian. Then shift back onto the right, begin exhaling, and push forward onto the left leg. From the

Figure 36. *Fourth movement (to the left):*
(A) *beginning,* (B) *farthest extension,* (C) *return.*

A

B

C

lower dan tian, the hands travel forward and separate as the arms reach maximum extension to the left. This closely resembles the portion of the butterfly stroke wherein the arms push the body out of the water. And, just as in the butterfly, when the arms reach maximum extension, the hands come together and pull in toward the body so that the process can be repeated. Repeat these actions twice before making the transition to the right, the footwork of which is identical to that described in the third movement.

It's important to note that while the arm and hand movements resemble the butterfly swim stroke, the breathing pattern of the fourth Qigong movement reverses that of the swim stroke. In swimming the butterfly, the swimmer inhales as the arms push the body out of the water, then exhales upon reentering when the hands are pulled toward the body. In the fourth movement, the exhale occurs as the arms extend, while the inhale coincides with the drawing in of the hands. In the case of the fourth movement,

Figure 37. *Fourth movement (to the right):*
(A) beginning, (B) farthest extention, (C) return.

A   B   C

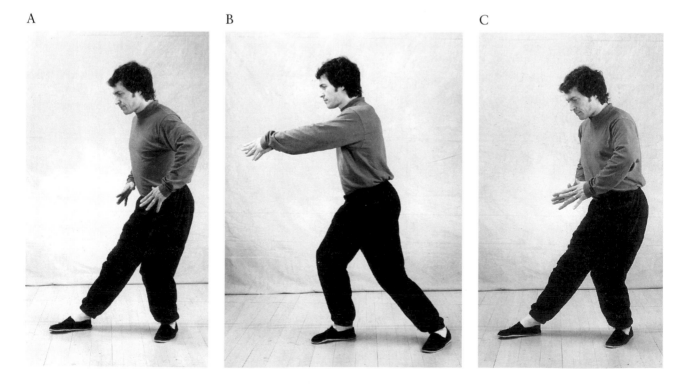

the metaphorical label shouldn't be taken too literally.

Together, the third and fourth movements engage the yang qi of the fu organs, as well as the qi of any food being digested and metabolized. These two movements enlist this yang qi to the greater purpose of contributing to a "critical mass," so to speak, of the collective qi derived from the spleen-pancreas and liver, which are also crucial to digestion. In terms of the Chinese paradigm, the order of the first four movements represents a progression from earth to wood to fire, indicated by the predominantly yang aspect of the fu organs. The transition from the second to the third and fourth movements suggests a change from ke to shen cycle, a change that is consummated in the fifth movement.

The fourth movement, like the third, also manipulates all three qi orbitals of dai mai and the lower portion of those of the middle dan tian, though the hands coax the orbits in the opposite direction of that of the third movement.

5. RAISING HANDS ALONG WITH STEPS (CATCH AND RELEASE)

The transition from the fourth to the fifth movement (figures 38 and 39) is a little more involved than previous transitions. After completing the third butterfly to the right and exhaling, begin inhaling and shift the weight from right to left by turning the waist so that the body is forward-facing. During this process, the feet must be adjusted as during the transitions of both the third and fourth movements. As the weight comes off the right foot and the waist turns, lift the toe of the right foot so that it can rotate to a forward-facing position, after which it can receive the body's weight without harming the knee. Once the weight is shifted onto the right, the left foot should be pointed to the left. These subtle movements should be done smoothly as one whole act, coordinated with one long inhale.

At the same time, the arms and hands, following the shifting weight, describe the lower half of a circle. They swing down across the front of the body and rise up so that the left extends, palm up, from the chest, while the right hovers, palm down, just beside the right side of the head. This movement resembles a famous movement from Chen-style Taiji called Part the Wild Horse's Mane, but I've given it the more West-friendly

140

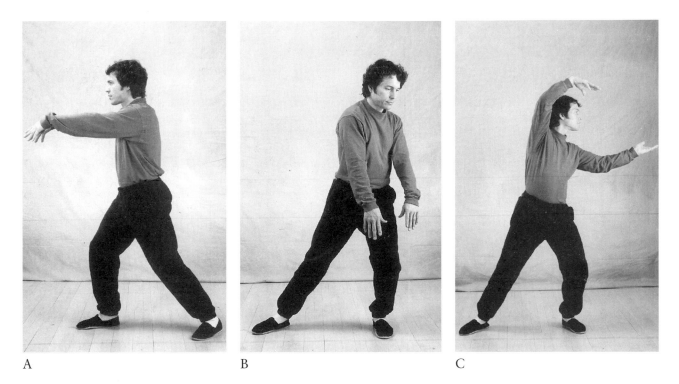

A B C

Figure 38. *Fifth movement (to the left): (A) transition from the fourth movement, (B) arms falling, (C) release, (D) catch, (E) release, (F) catch.*

D E F

A   B   C

Figure 39. *Fifth movement (to the right):*
(A) *release,* (B) *hands overhead,* (C) *release,* (D) *catch,* (E) *release.*

name Catch and Release, because the hands swing into position as though
they were catching a large, weightless ball, which they subsequently release. As in the other movements, each phase correlates to the breath.
Inhales coincide with the catch phase of the movement, while exhales ac-
company the release phase.

The first portion of the fifth movement begins from a catch position
(inhale), then flows forward into a release (exhale), during which the
weight shifts from the right foot onto the left. The hands follow the shifting weight, the wrists flexing slightly as though about to let go of the large,
weightless ball, but once the left leg takes on sixty to seventy percent of
the body's weight, the inhale begins again, and the waist turns forty-five
degrees back to the right, which shifts the weight back onto the right leg.
The hands respond by reassuming their "catch" position. Repeat these
movements two more times.

142

D   E

The transition to the right side completes the upper half of the circle begun with the transition from fourth to fifth movements. From a leftward release position (exhale), begin inhaling and shift the weight from left to right, rotating ninety degrees on the heel of the left foot and turning the waist to a forward-facing position. At the same time, swing the hands overhead and lower them into an apparent release position before shifting the weight back onto the left leg and pointing the right foot to the right, at which point the hands settle into a catch position. From here, execute a release and slowly exhale. Do this two more times.

The fifth movement draws upon heart and pericardium qi, the fire element. The small spark ignited when the yang fire of the third and fourth movements meets the wood of the second is brought into full flame. The shift from the ke to the shen paradigm is complete. The body's qi has now traveled from a creator element (wood) to its creation (fire).

While the transitions from fourth to fifth, and from the left side to the right, involve blending the qi orbitals of all three dan tians, the catch and release phases of the movement appear focused on the middle and upper dan tians. The hand movements seem to have progressed from the lower to the upper dan tian.

6. PUTTING HANDS ABOVE EYES
(STOOP AND GATHER, STAND AND DISPERSE)

The sixth movement (figures 40 and 41) and the seventh movement (figures 42 and 43) are related in a number of ways. Though I treat them separately here for the sake of presenting them clearly, I shall first focus on their similarities.

In terms of what the legs do, the sixth and seventh movements are the same. They involve a stooping action, followed by standing up straight on one leg, lifting the knee of the empty leg up into the chest: a movement inspired by the crane, an ancient symbol of health and longevity in Chinese mythology, martial arts, and Qigong. The formal name for the seventh move—Big Bird Relaxing Its Wings—is surely a reference to the crane. As for the breath, exhales occur during the stoop, inhales during the standing up. Both the actions of the legs and the breathing are a constant throughout both the sixth and seventh moves. Only the motion of the hands and arms differs.

As in all the transitions from right to left, the transition from the last of the fifth movements into the sixth involves a weight shift on the inhale from right to left. Before the whole body turns back toward the left, however, the left foot, which has been forward-facing, must turn forty-five degrees to the left, which becomes the basic orientation of the body. The left leg then accepts most of the body's weight, while the right empties, resting on the toe to assist with balance. At the same time, the arms drop from the release posture of the fifth move to cross in front of the lower dan tian, left hand on the inside, from where they rise over the head. From this posture the actual sixth movement, which has two phases, begins.

The first phase of the sixth move I call Stoop and Gather, during which the exhale occurs. As the arms drop from overhead, the left support leg

Figure 40. *Sixth movement (to the left): (A) release, (B) gather transition, (C) disperse, (D) gather, (E) disperse, (F) drop leg.*

144

A

B

C

D

E

F

A   B

Figure 41. *Sixth movement (to the right):*
(A) *step right,* (B) *gather* (C) *disperse,* (D) *drop leg.*

bends, arms crossing at the wrists, left hand inside, as though scooping up
a pile of leaves. The second phase, called Stand and Disperse, initiates the
inhale. First, stand upright, straightening the left support leg and lifting
the right knee up into the abdomen. At the same time, bring the arms up
overhead and separate them in a dispersing gesture, as though scattering
the leaves just scooped up in the arms. Immediately after the arms separate, drop the right leg so that it gently returns to its touching position.
Repeat both phases of the movement two more times.

C

D

Transition to the right side occurs during the Stand and Disperse phase of the third repetition. On the inhale, instead of dropping the lifted right leg, gently move it to the right, making sure that the right foot lands in a position forty-five degrees right of forward-facing. Now the roles of the legs are reversed. The right leg now provides support, while the left leg rests on its toe to serve as balance. Then, on the exhale, stoop and gather, after which stand and disperse on the inhale. Repeat the whole movement two more times.

A   B

Figure 42. *Seventh movement (to the left): (A) step left and gather overhead, (B) stoop, and disperse, (C) stand and lift leg, (D) drop leg.*

7. BIG BIRD RELAXING ITS WINGS
(STOOP AND DISPERSE, STAND AND GATHER)

The last move of the sixth movement flows naturally into the first of the seventh movement. Instead of standing to disperse for the third time to the right, inhale and step left onto the left foot in the same fashion as in the sixth movement, emptying the right leg. Crossing the hands overhead, left inside, as though gathering air, exhale and stoop on the left leg, separating the arms in a dispersing motion. On the inhale, stand and lift the

148

C

D

right knee into the abdomen, then drop it to its original position as the hands cross overhead as before. After stooping to disperse, repeat the whole action only once more.

After the Stoop and Disperse phase of the last of the repetitions to the left, stand up on the inhale and raise the right knee, but instead of dropping it beside the left, set it in its former sixth-movement spot on the right. Empty the left and let it rest on the toe beside the right. At the same time, gather the arms overhead and follow out the same stoop-disperse-exhale, stand-gather-inhale actions to the right. Aside from weight distribution of the legs, the only difference here is that the right hand, instead of the left, will be on the inside.

149

A   B

Figure 43. *Seventh movement (to the right):* (A) *step right, and gather overhead,* (B) *stoop and disperse,* (C) *stand and lift leg,* (D) *drop leg.*

From earlier discussion you should recognize that both the sixth and seventh movements invoke primarily the lungs and to a lesser extent the kidneys. Like the third and fourth movements, which promote the digestive organs, the sixth and seventh moves resemble one another, differing only in the patterns of the arm motion. And, just as the third and fourth movements help spread the qi of the lower to the middle dan tian, so do the sixth and seventh function on the more general level of spreading the growing mass of collective qi from head to toe and vice versa. We have

C

D

now left the shen cycle and returned to that of the ke: the movements follow the natural order from the controller (fire) to the controlled (metal), a reversal of the order established between the left-handed movements of the first and second (earth, controlled) and the right-handed movements of the first and second (liver, controller).

As for the qi orbitals of the three dan tians, the sixth and seventh movements clearly mingle the belts of all three dan tians by stooping, during which the three energy centers are compressed. The whole movement, however, seems more concerned with the interplay between the upper and lower dan tians, and the up and down movements of the arms suggest that the diagonal orbitals are affected primarily.

Both the stooping and crane postures tie the sixth and seventh movements solidly to the eighth, which most directly invokes the kidney's energy. As I pointed out earlier, when the body is bent, the lower abdomen compresses, perhaps exerting pressure on the kidneys and causing a jing secretion, which is then encouraged into the whole system by the more expansive portions of the sixth and seventh movements. Moreover, when the knee lifts and presses into the abdomen, each kidney is alternately "squeezed" or massaged, perhaps further encouraging jing to be secreted so that it can be circulated and used for rejuvenation. Chinese doctors and Qigong masters have long speculated that this could be one explanation for the crane's peculiar penchant for standing on one leg and folding the other into its abdomen.

8. SWALLOW PLAYING WITH WATER
(UP AND DOWN, SEPARATE AND TOGETHER)

Unlike the others, the eighth movement (figure 44) is done only in a forward-facing direction; but like the others, the eighth coordinates bending and straightening the legs with the arm and hand motions. The transition from the seventh to the eighth occurs after the third Stand and Gather movement to the right. After inhaling, let the arms and hands fall gently to the sides and slowly straighten the knees. This puts you back in the position from which the Qigong movements began.

In fact, the first phase of the eighth move—called here Up and Down—mirrors the opening Qigong movement. On the inhale, simply raise the arms, which should be straight without tension, to the level of the collarbone. The hands should be relaxed and bent at the wrist. This is the up part of the Up and Down phase. Then, on the exhale, bend elbows, wrists, and knees, and bring the hands down just as in the opening move.

The second phase—Separate and Together—resembles playing an accordion. It begins when the hands reach the upper portion of the lower dan tian. At that point, begin a slow inhale, turn the palms so that they face each other, then draw the hands apart as though filling the accordion with air. At the same time, slowly straighten the knees. Then, on the exhale, gently press the hands together in the manner of playing an accor-

Figure 44. *Eighth movement:* (A) *begin,* (B) *up,* (C) *down,* (D) *separate,* (E) *together,* (F) *finish.*

dion and bend the knees. When the hands are several inches apart, drop them to the middle of the lower dan tian. From there the up portion of the Up and Down phase begins, concomitant with inhaling and straightening the knees.

After the third repetition of the eighth move, let the hands drop. The eight formal movements are complete.

As discussed earlier, the eighth movement activates the kidneys, the water element. Thus the transition from seventh to eighth again directs the process from the ke to the shen cycle, from metal (creator) to water (created). As for which dan tians and orbitals are involved, the movements focus exclusively on blending the orbitals of all three dan tians.

In order to understand why the kidneys are reserved for the last move, it is important to remember the primacy that Chinese medicine places on kidney qi and its relation to overall health. The Chinese interpretation of "kidney" doesn't match that of Western medicine, which usually draws on the heavily mechanical metaphor of a "blood purification plant" to explain the kidneys' function. Though the Western model sees the kidneys as vital organs, the traditional Chinese view imbues the kidney system with far more significance. They are the seat of procreation, health, and longevity. The Chinese medical mosaic also puts far more emphasis on the role of sexuality in the condition of the kidneys, because in the Chinese paradigm "sex" always means jing, the body's most precious qi. Thus it is reasonable to assume that without careful safeguarding, kidney qi cannot accrue a sufficient quantity to sustain a significant Qigong effect. As mentioned previously, the kidneys are believed to store jing, the body's most precious form of qi, adding even greater weight to the growing collective pool of qi generated by the previous movements.

The eighth movement consummates the qi-gathering movements of the Three Emperors Qigong. It distributes the qi soup blended and cooked up over the course of the previous seven movements, and especially infuses lao gong. By the end of the third kidney move, the totality of the body's qi fills the hands and radiates from palm to palm. You are ready for the next stage.

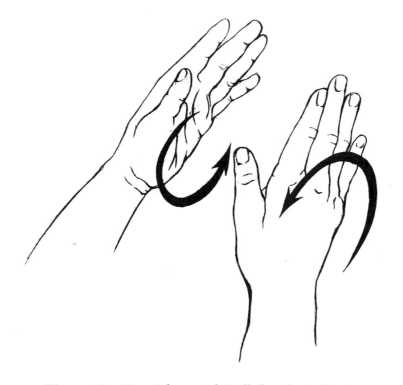

Figure 45. *Tiger Plays with Ball (hands circling).*

Standing Meditation and Tiger Plays with Ball

After completing the last of the eighth movements, raise the hands into the gentle embracing posture described in chapter 7. Remember to keep the spine erect without being stiff and the legs straight without being taut. Relax the elbows downward toward the rib cage. Close the eyes and do reverse breathing (tongue still curled) for five minutes. If the arms become unbearably tired, shorten the time to two or three minutes. If dizzy or unable to stand, perform the meditation while seated.

After holding the embracing posture for two to five minutes, try the Tiger Plays with Ball exercise, also described in chapter 7. To recapitulate, let the palms face one another, as though holding a beach ball between the palms, then slowly begin to rotate the hands in forward, alternating circles. After a minute or so, reverse the circles. You should feel heat, tingles, or a magnetic sensation radiating from one palm to the other. Tingles or prickles indicate sick qi, which in itself isn't anything to worry about. All people have sick qi. If you suffer from some chronic disease or are afflicted physically or mentally, however, the sensation should be taken as a warning. The best advice I can give such people is to find a good teacher without delay and begin working on your health.

After two to five minutes of "playing with the ball," lower the hands to the sides, then do three Marrow Washing motions, depicted in chapter 7 (see page 00). Also remember that women should place their right hands and men their left hands closest to their bodies.

Dai Mai and Jian Mai

After following the above routine for at least a month, practicing twice daily (morning and evening before meals are the best times), you can experiment with the automatic movements of dai mai and jian mai. A word of warning, however, about such experimenting. First, under no circumstances should anyone do hard automatic movements without having worked with a qualified Qigong teacher for a period of time. Second, even the milder automatic movements of dai mai or jian mai can produce unexpected physical or emotional results. More frequently the unexpected results are emotional. Many of my students have had odd feelings well up that run the gamut from ecstasy to depression. Of course, negative feelings are the things to watch for. In the event that you have such an experience, discontinue practice and seek help through either a mental health professional or a Qigong teacher; I usually recommend seeing both. I have had great success in working with students who also work with psychotherapists. A euphoric feeling can also cause trouble, especially if the student tries to induce the feeling repeatedly. Several of my students have been able to generate "orgasmic" feelings by practicing Qigong, and, given the Western attitude toward orgasm, it was no wonder that they tried to have these feelings as often as possible. The result, of course, is a loss of qi, perhaps even a loss of jing.

Physical aberrations are also possible. For example, the most common low-grade affliction from which people suffer is the upper respiratory infection. Many of my students who have been diagnosed with "allergies" or "chronic fatigue syndrome" or "bad colds" have experienced skin rashes after practicing Qigong. Since the skin is considered an aspect of the lung system, such a reaction makes perfect sense. But having a "respiratory infection" manifest itself on the body's surface (for all to see!) can be unnerving. If having such a reaction frightens you, then discontinue practice. If you are not afraid, keep practicing. The appearance of a rash means your internal qi has driven the invading sick qi to the outer realms of your body. A rash may actually signify a small victory in the battle for health.

Chapter 7 describes my experiences with both the "belt" and "shoulder" energetic orbitals. You should begin as I did: by engaging dai mai, after a minute or two of playing with the ball (the eight formal movements and the standing meditation having been completed as well). Lower the hands so that the palms face the lower dan tian. You should feel sensations that are the same as or similar to what you feel when you play with the ball. Next circle the hands in front of dan tian and keep circling as you turn the waist to the left; then continue circling as you turn back to the right. If you don't feel anything, go back to playing with the ball. If you feel qi or some indication of qi, then you have engaged dai mai. Use the hands to give dai mai a spin; then, as though hula-hooping in slow motion, rotate the hips in a circle while you hold the hands in front of the lower dan tian. You should feel qi fluxing between the hands. Close the eyes, relax, and enjoy the sensation, and eventually give in to the sense that the hips are being moved by the revolutions of the invisible orbitals.

Again, if any adverse or disturbing results occur, stop and Marrow Wash three times. If all goes well, continue playing with dai mai for eight to ten minutes. At the end of that time, bring all motion to a slow halt, open the eyes, and Marrow Wash three times.

After three or four weeks of playing with dai mai, you may want to graduate to jian mai. You should engage the shoulder orbitals after five minutes of standing meditation. Open the eyes, exhale, and bring the fingers close together without touching, then inhale and spread the hands apart. Next rotate the hands as in Tiger Plays with Ball. If all goes well, both arms should feel thick with qi. Move the hands up to the face, then above the head, and your hands should feel changes in the qi field as you

A   B

Figure 46. *Postures used in sitting meditation.*

proceed into the orbitals of the upper dan tian. Then lower the hands to their original position, close the eyes, and begin circling the hands by moving both arms at the shoulder, a motion, you may remember, called tiao dong, *dong* meaning "action," and *tiao* referring to a long stick held across the shoulders, used for carrying pails of water. By allowing the upper body to engage in tiao dong and by simultaneously moving the hips according to dai mai, the whole body should feel encased in a moving mass of qi. When the arms grow fatigued, lower them and move by dai

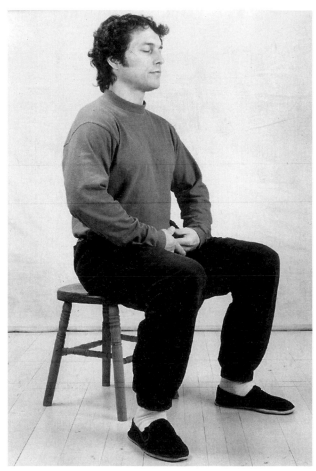

C

D

mai. Move them back to feel jian mai when the impulse to do so occurs. You should move in this fashion, with eyes closed, for about ten minutes, at the end of which you may open your eyes and Marrow Wash three times.

Again, should any disturbing reaction occur, discontinue what you are doing and do three Marrow Washings. In such an event, you must scale back your Qigong practice to a more elementary level or find a good teacher (whose system will most likely involve learning different movements, etc.) or quit practicing altogether. My advice is to seek out a capable teacher.

Sitting Meditation

After a session of moving Qigong (dong gong), you should conclude with unmoving Qigong (jing gong). The same warnings given under the previous heading apply here. In fact, as far as emotional reactions are concerned, sitting meditation is more likely to provoke a response. Should that happen, pursue the same options for remedies outlined previously.

Sitting meditation may be done in any of four postures: full lotus, half-lotus, or Indian style. (Alternatively, one can sit on a chair.) Choose a sitting position, on either the floor or the edge of a chair, that is comfortable. During jing gong, relaxation is most important. Keeping the posture erect without being rigid, head held up as though by a thin wire suspended from the ceiling, curl the tongue and practice reverse breathing. To keep the mind disciplined, imagine the thin red line running from the center of the lower dan tian to that of the upper dan tian. On the inhale, the red line ascends to the upper dan tian's center, and on the exhale the line falls back into the midst of the lower dan tian. If thoughts enter your mind, don't drive them out forcefully. Allow them to linger for a moment, then, when their hold on you seems to abate, go back to the image of the red line.

If you aren't used to sitting meditation, begin with five- or ten-minute sessions. As your concentration and comfort levels increase, however, lengthen the time to a full twenty minutes. At the end of each session, open the eyes slowly and rub the palms together. Then press the palms into the eyes and wipe down the entire face three times.

If you begin to experience heat or a sense of fullness in the lower dan tian, then your Qigong practice is working. You should approach each session with conviction and try to practice at least twice daily. Should you experience movement in the lower dan tian region, such as a pulsing sensation, then you are, as the Chinese say, "one of the lucky ones." That is to say you have some special moral or qi qualities that make Qigong practice effective for you. If you are a "lucky one," then your pursuit of enlightenment and health through Qigong should be all the more determined.

If your response to Qigong practice is lackluster or negligible, you need to find a good teacher. I commend all to this effort, and I hope that you can find a teacher as excellent as Zhang Jinwei. If you find such a teacher, show gratitude and respect, and work hard to bring others to this rich and astounding practice of the Middle Kingdom.

REFERENCES

ALITTO, GUY S. *The Last Confucian.* Berkeley: University of California Press, 1979.

BROWN, DAVID. "A Hands-Off Approach to Healing." *Washington Post,* 3 September 1993: B1.

BUTTERFIELD, FOX. *Alive in the Bitter Sea.* London: Hodder and Stroughton, 1982.

CHANG, STEPHEN. *The Complete Book of Acupuncture.* Berkeley: Celestial Arts, 1976.

———. *The Great Tao.* San Francisco: Tao Publishing, 1992.

CHOPRA, DEEPAK. *Quantum Healing.* New York: Bantam Books, 1990.

DENG, MING-DAO. *The Scholar Warrior: An Introduction to the Tao of Everyday Life.* San Francisco: HarperSanFrancisco, 1990.

———. *The Wandering Taoist.* New York: Harper and Row, 1986.

EISENBERG, DAVID. *Encounters with Qi.* New York: Penguin Books, 1987.

Essentials of Chinese Acupuncture. Beijing: Foreign Languages Press, 1980.

FISH, KEN. "The Nature of Chi." *Internal Strength,* July 1993: 4–5.

FLAWS, BOB. *Free and Easy: Traditional Chinese Gynecology for American Women.* 2nd ed. Boulder, Colo.: Blue Poppy Press, 1990.

HAMMER, LEON. *Dragon Rises / Red Bird Flies.* Barrytown, N.Y.: Station Hill Press, 1990.

Healing and the Mind with Bill Moyers: The Mystery of Chi (video tape). Dir. Gary Grubin. Ambrose Video Publishing, Inc., 1993.

KAPTCHUK, TED. *The Web that Has No Weaver.* Boston: Congdon and Weed, 1984.

KORZYBSKI, ALFRED. *Science and Sanity.* 4th ed. Lakeville, Conn.: International Non-Aristotelian Library Publishing Company, 1980.

RAHULA, WALPOLA. *What the Buddha Taught.* New York: Grove Weidenfeld, 1974.

REID, DANIEL P. *Chinese Herbal Medicine.* Boston: Shambhala Publications, 1987.

TAUBES, GARY. "An Electrifying Possibility." *Discover,* April 1986: 23–37.

Tibetan Medical Paintings. Vol. 1. New York: Serindia Publications, 1992.

VARENNE, JEAN. *Yoga and the Hindu Tradition.* Trans. Derek Coltman. Chicago: University of Chicago Press, 1976.

YAN XIN. *Yan Xin and the Contemporary Sciences.* Trans. Jo Ann Wozniak et al. International Yan Xin Qigong Association, 1991.

YOGANANDA, PARAMAHANSA. *Autobiography of a Yogi.* Los Angeles: Self-Realization Fellowship, 1993.

INDEX

Please note that page numbers of illustrations are italicized. The eight movements of Three Emperors Qigong are listed under that heading in order of practice.